Fatty Liver Diet Cookbook

The Most Complete Step-By-Step Guide with 365 Days of Healthy Recipes to Purify Your Liver to Regain Health and Energy. Up to 5 Ingredients to Cook in 30 Mins or Less

By

Alex Mc Corner

Contents

Introduction

Welcome to the "Fatty Liver Cookbook: Nourishing Your Liver, One Delicious Bite at a Time." This cookbook is designed to be your comprehensive guide to understanding and managing fatty liver disease through the power of nutrition and wholesome cooking.

In the following pages, we'll delve into the various aspects of fatty liver disease, helping you grasp the intricacies of this condition. We'll explore the causes and risk factors, from genetics to lifestyle choices, shedding light on why it's become a pressing health concern worldwide.

Understanding Fatty Liver Disease, Causes and Risk Factors

Fatty liver disease, also known as hepatic steatosis, is a common condition characterized by the accumulation of excess fat in the liver cells.

It is a multifaceted condition with various underlying causes and risk factors contributing to its development. A deeper understanding of these factors is essential for effectively managing the condition.

Causes of Fatty Liver Disease

1. **Non-Alcoholic Fatty Liver Disease (NAFLD):**

   - **Insulin Resistance:** One of the primary drivers of NAFLD is insulin resistance, which leads to increased fat storage in liver cells.

   - **Obesity:** Excess body weight, particularly abdominal obesity, significantly contributes to NAFLD.

   - **Metabolic Syndrome:** NAFLD is often associated with metabolic syndrome, a cluster of conditions including high blood pressure, high blood sugar, and abnormal cholesterol levels.

   - **Genetics:** Some individuals may be genetically predisposed to developing fatty liver disease.

2. **Alcoholic Fatty Liver Disease (AFLD):**

   - **Excessive Alcohol Consumption:** AFLD is directly caused by chronic, heavy alcohol consumption. Alcohol is processed by the liver, which means that drinking to excess might back up the liver's ability to process fat.

Risk Factors for Fatty Liver Disease

1. **Dietary Factors:**

   - **High Sugar Intake:** Diets rich in sugary foods and beverages can contribute to the development of fatty liver disease.

   - **Unhealthy Fats:** A diet high in saturated and trans fats can promote fat buildup in the liver.

2. **Lifestyle Choices:**

   - **Physical Inactivity:** A sedentary lifestyle can contribute to obesity and insulin resistance, increasing the risk of fatty liver disease.

   - **Rapid Weight Loss:** Drastic weight loss methods can release stored fat in the liver, exacerbating the condition.

3. **Medical Conditions:**
   - **Type 2 Diabetes:** People with diabetes are at a higher risk of developing NAFLD due to insulin resistance.
   - **High Blood Pressure:** Hypertension can increase the risk of liver disease.
   - **High Cholesterol:** Elevated cholesterol levels may be associated with NAFLD.
4. **Medications and Supplements:**
   - Some medications and supplements, including corticosteroids and certain antiviral drugs, may contribute to liver fat accumulation.
5. **Other Factors:**
   - **Age:** NAFLD is more common in middle-aged and older adults.
   - **Gender:** Men are generally at a higher risk of developing fatty liver disease than women.
   - **Ethnicity:** Some ethnic groups have a higher predisposition to NAFLD.
6. **Environmental Factors:**
   - **Toxic Exposures:** Exposure to environmental toxins and pollutants can impact liver health.

Understanding these causes and risk factors is the first step in taking control of your liver health. By identifying the factors that apply to you, you can make informed choices about your lifestyle, diet, and overall health management to reduce your risk or effectively manage existing fatty liver disease.

Importance of Diet

One of the most powerful tools at your disposal for managing and even reversing fatty liver disease is your diet. What you eat plays a pivotal role in the health of your liver, making dietary choices a crucial component of your journey toward liver wellness.

In this cookbook, we'll embark on a culinary adventure together, discovering the foods that can promote a healthier liver and those you should limit or avoid. You'll find diverse recipes, meal plans, and tips to make eating for liver health a flavorful and enjoyable experience.

A Holistic Approach

Managing fatty liver disease is not solely about eliminating certain foods from your diet. It's about embracing a holistic approach to wellness. This includes nourishing your body with the right nutrients, exercising, managing stress, and making sustainable lifestyle changes.

Throughout the book, we'll emphasize the importance of maintaining a balanced and liver-friendly lifestyle. We'll guide exercise routines, stress reduction techniques, and smart cooking practices to support your liver health journey.

By completing this cookbook, you'll have a repertoire of delicious and nutritious recipes and a deeper understanding of your health and the tools to take control of it. You'll be equipped to make informed decisions about your diet, knowing that each meal can be a step towards a healthier liver and a happier, more vibrant you.

So, let's begin this journey together. Turn the page, grab your apron, and let's cook up some liver-loving goodness that will nourish your body and put you on the path to optimal liver health. Your liver will thank you, and your taste buds will be in for a treat!

Chapter 1: Eating Right for a Healthy Liver

1.1 Liver-Friendly Foods

When promoting liver health, the right choice of foods can make a significant difference. Incorporating liver-friendly foods into your diet can help reduce fat buildup in the liver, support its functions, and enhance overall well-being.

Lean Proteins: Lean protein sources are essential for a healthy liver. They provide the amino acids necessary for liver detoxification and repair. Opt for:

- **Skinless Poultry:** Chicken and turkey breast are excellent choices.
- **Fish:** Fatty fish like salmon, mackerel, and trout are rich in omega-3 fatty acids, which have anti-inflammatory properties.
- **Plant-Based Proteins:** Legumes, tofu, and tempeh are great options for vegetarians and vegans.

Whole Grains: Whole grains are packed with fiber and nutrients, making them valuable to a liver-friendly diet. They help stabilize blood sugar levels and prevent excessive insulin production. Include:

- **Brown Rice:** A fiber-rich alternative to white rice.
- **Quinoa:** A complete protein source with a nutty flavor.
- **Oats:** High in soluble fiber, oats support digestive health.

Fresh Fruits and Vegetables: Colorful fruits and vegetables provide essential antioxidants, vitamins, and minerals that benefit liver health. Aim for a variety of:

- **Leafy Greens:** Spinach, kale, and collard greens are rich in antioxidants.
- **Berries:** Blueberries, strawberries, and raspberries are high in anthocyanins.
- **Citrus Fruits:** Oranges, lemons, and grapefruits supply vitamin C.

Healthy Fats: While you should limit fat intake, healthy fats are crucial for nutrient absorption and overall well-being. Opt for:

- **Avocado:** Packed with monounsaturated fats and fiber.
- **Nuts and Seeds:** Almonds, walnuts, chia seeds, and flaxseeds provide healthy fats and protein.
- **Olive Oil:** Extra virgin olive oil is rich in antioxidants.

1.2 Foods to Avoid

Knowing which foods to avoid to prevent further liver damage and fat accumulation is just as important as incorporating liver-friendly foods.

Sugary Foods and Beverages: Excessive sugar intake can lead to insulin resistance and contribute to fatty liver disease. Limit or avoid:

- **Soda:** High in added sugars and empty calories.
- **Candies:** Often contain refined sugars and artificial additives.

- **Processed Snacks:** Cookies, cakes, and pastries are typically high in sugar.

Saturated and Trans Fats: Saturated and trans fats are detrimental to liver health as they can increase bad cholesterol levels and promote inflammation. Steer clear of:

- **Fried Foods:** Fried chicken, French fries, and fried snacks.
- **Processed Meats:** Bacon, sausages, and hot dogs are high in saturated fats.
- **Trans Fat-Containing Foods:** Check labels for partially hydrogenated oils.

High-Sodium Foods: Excess salt intake can contribute to fluid retention and high blood pressure, potentially worsening liver health. Reduce consumption of:

- **Canned Soups:** Many are loaded with sodium.
- **Processed Meats:** Deli meats often contain added salt.
- **Fast Food:** High-sodium content is common in fast-food items.

By making informed choices and incorporating liver-friendly foods while avoiding those that can harm your liver, you'll be taking a significant step towards managing and improving the health of your liver. In the chapters ahead, we'll explore delicious recipes and meal plans that align with these dietary principles, making nourishing your liver and boosting your overall well-being easier than ever.

1.3 Balancing Macronutrients

Balancing macronutrients—protein, carbohydrates, and fats—is fundamental to creating nutritious and satisfying meals that promote liver health.

Protein: Protein is essential for repairing and maintaining liver cells. Incorporating lean protein sources into your meals helps support liver function and promotes a feeling of fullness. Consider:

- **Poultry:** Skinless chicken or turkey breast.
- **Fish:** Fatty fish like salmon or trout for omega-3s.
- **Plant-Based Options:** Legumes, tofu, and tempeh for vegetarians.

Carbohydrates: Carbohydrates provide energy and are vital to a balanced diet. However, choosing the right carbs is crucial for liver health. Opt for complex carbohydrates that provide sustained energy without causing rapid blood sugar spikes:

- **Whole Grains:** Brown rice, quinoa, and whole wheat pasta.
- **Fiber-Rich Foods:** Vegetables, fruits, and legumes.
- **Moderation:** Keep portion sizes in check to manage blood sugar levels.

Fats: Healthy fats are necessary for nutrient absorption and overall health. Focus on unsaturated fats and avoid saturated and trans fats:

- **Healthy Fats:** Avocado, nuts, seeds, and olive oil.
- **Limit Saturated Fats:** Reduce consumption of fatty meats and full-fat dairy.
- **Avoid Trans Fats:** Check labels for partially hydrogenated oils.

Balancing these macronutrients in your meals helps provide a well-rounded and nutritionally rich diet that supports liver health. By paying attention to portion sizes and the quality of the foods you consume, you can create meals that are satisfying, nourishing, and conducive to managing fatty liver disease.

Chapter 2: Meal Planning. How to Build a One-Week Meal Plan

Creating a practical and balanced meal plan is essential for successfully managing fatty liver disease. In this chapter, we provide sample meal plans and a one-week meal plan to serve as a foundation for your journey to liver health.

2.1 Building a One-Week Meal Plan for Liver Health

Creating a one-week meal plan tailored to liver health requires thoughtful consideration of macronutrients, portion sizes, and nutrient-rich ingredients. Here's a step-by-step guide to help you build a balanced and liver-friendly one-week meal plan:

Step 1: Determine Your Caloric Needs

Before you start planning meals, calculate your daily caloric needs. Age, gender, activity level, and weight goals influence calorie requirements. You can use an online calculator or consult a registered dietitian for a personalized estimate.

Step 2: Set Nutrient Goals

Establish nutrient goals for your meal plan, including the following:

- **Protein:** Aim for a moderate amount of lean protein sources like poultry, fish, legumes, or tofu in each meal.

- **Carbohydrates:** Prioritize complex carbohydrates like whole grains, vegetables, and fruits, and consider your daily fiber intake.

- **Fats:** Focus on healthy fats from sources like avocados, nuts, seeds, and olive oil while limiting saturated and trans fats.

- **Fiber:** Incorporate fiber-rich foods to support digestion and manage blood sugar levels.

- **Vitamins and Minerals:** Ensure a variety of colorful fruits and vegetables to provide essential vitamins and minerals.

- **Hydration:** Include adequate water intake throughout the day.

Step 3: Plan Your Meals

Break down your meal plan into three main meals (breakfast, lunch, and dinner) and snacks. Here's how to structure each meal:

Monday

- **Breakfast:** Gluten-Free Breakfast Pancakes
- **Lunch:** Chicken Patties
- **Dinner:** Garlic and Thyme Chicken Thighs
- **Snacks/Sweets:** Low-Carb Chocolate Almond Slice

Tuesday

- **Breakfast:** Pumpkin Pancakes
- **Lunch:** Roasted Turkey Drumsticks
- **Dinner:** Mediterranean Beef Skewers
- **Snacks/Sweets:** Min Nectarine Ice-Cream

Wednesday

- **Breakfast:** Pumpkin and Olive Frittata
- **Lunch:** Easy Lemon Baked Salmon
- **Dinner:** Lamb Cutlets with Peach Salad
- **Snacks/Sweets:** Crunchy Oat and Nut Bars

Thursday

- **Breakfast:** Gluten Free Cinnamon Rice Porridge
- **Lunch:** Simple Baked Salmon
- **Dinner:** Dairy-Free Lemon and Mustard Turkey Thighs
- **Snacks/Sweets:** Dark Chocolate Truffles

Friday

- **Breakfast:** Mushroom and Onion Omelet
- **Lunch:** Low-Carb Salmon Salad
- **Dinner:** Zucchini and Salmon Slice
- **Snacks/Sweets:** Gluten-Free Coffee Protein Balls

Saturday

- **Breakfast:** Apple and Cinnamon Quinoa Porridge
- **Lunch:** Roast Cauliflower and Quinoa Salad
- **Dinner:** Baked Salmon with Avocado Salad
- **Snacks/Sweets:**

Sunday

- **Breakfast:** Dairy-Free Blueberry Pancakes
- **Lunch:** Grilled Tuna Steaks
- **Dinner:** Low-Carb Garlic & Rosemary Chicken Thighs
- **Snacks/Sweets:** Cacao And Almond Smoothie Bowl

Step 4: Create a Shopping List

List all the ingredients you'll need for your planned meals and snacks. This helps you stay organized and ensure everything is ready to prepare your meals throughout the week.

Step 5: Prep and Cook

Allocate time for meal preparation. Pre-chop vegetables, marinate proteins, or batch-cook grains and legumes to streamline weekly cooking. Having prepared ingredients readily available makes sticking to your meal plan more manageable.

Step 6: Monitor & Adjust

Keep track of how you feel during the week concerning your eating plan. Take note of changes in your vitality, digestion, or general health. Adjust portion sizes or ingredients to meet your specific dietary goals and preferences.

Step 7: Repeat and Customize

After completing your one-week meal plan, you can repeat it or use it as a template for future weeks. Customize it by incorporating different recipes, ingredients, and flavors to keep your meals exciting and varied.

Remember that consistency is key to supporting liver health, so aim to create meal plans that align with your nutritional goals and are sustainable over the long term. Consulting with a healthcare professional or registered dietitian can provide personalized guidance based on your needs and health status.

Chapter 3: Delicious Breakfasts for Liver Health

Here are some best breakfast Recipes to Purify Your Liver to Regain Health and Energy.

3.1 Gluten-Free Breakfast Pancakes

Prep Time: 10 Mins, Cook Time: 15 Mins, Servings: 1

Ingredients

- 2 large eggs
- ½ cup Olive oil & cottage cheese
- ½ cup oats gluten-free
- 6 sliced olives
- ½ tsp oregano dried

Method

- Blend or process the cottage cheese, oats, and egg until completely smooth. Combine everything else (except the oil) and stir it in.
- Prepare a pan with medium heat. Include the olive oil. Pour in the pancake batter. The back of the spoon may be used to distribute the mixture if necessary. Before flipping the food over to cook the additional side, wait for bubbles to form.

Nutritional Facts: Calories: 4.1 Kcal, Protein: 0.1 g, Carbs: 0.8 g, Fats: 0.1 g

3.2 Gluten Free Cinnamon Rice Porridge

Prep Time: 10 Mins, Cook Time: 20 Mins, Servings: 2

Ingredients

- 1 cup cooked rice
- 1 & ¼ cups of milk
- 4 pitted Medjool dates
- ¼ tsp of cinnamon
- 1 tsp natural sugar

Method

- In a saucepan, mix everything except the fresh fruit and almonds. Start a boil using.
- Simmer for 5–8 mins, stirring occasionally, or until thickened.
- Put the mixture into two dishes and garnish with the added fruit and nuts.

Nutritional Facts: Calories: 133 Kcal, Protein: 2 g, Carbs: 29 g, Fats: 0.5 g

3.3 Apple and Cinnamon Quinoa Porridge

Prep Time: 10 Mins, Cook Time: 10 Mins, Servings: 2

Ingredients

- 2 cups milk coconut
- ½ cup of quinoa
- 2 coarsely grated apples
- ½ tsp of cinnamon
- 1 tbsp protein powder whey

Method

- Quinoa has to be soaked in water for 12 hours. The next day, empty the water and give it a good rinsing.
- Cook the quinoa & milk together above low heat till the quinoa is tender and the milk has thickened.
- Add the rest of the ingredients to the porridge and mix well.

Nutritional Facts: Calories: 368 Kcal, Protein: 2.8 g, Carbs: 17.8 g, Fats: 0.8 g

3.4 Dairy-Free Blueberry Pancakes

Prep Time: 05 Mins, Cook Time: 20 Mins, Servings: 3

Ingredients

- 2 lightly whisked large eggs
- 2 tbsps oil olive
- 1 cup meal almond
- 1 tsp each of vanilla extract & powder baking
- ½ cup of blueberries

Method

- In a dish, mix everything except the blueberries until thoroughly combined. Wait 10 mins before stirring again. Blend the blueberries into the sauce.
- Olive oil should be heated in a pan over moderate heat.
- Fry the pancakes till golden on one side. To finish cooking, turn the meat over.
- Serve.

Nutritional Facts: Calories: 340 Kcal, Protein: 7.8 g, Carbs: 39.2 g, Fats: 17.7 g

3.5 Easy Almond Butter Overnight Oats

Prep Time: 05 Mins, Cook Time: 30 Mins, Servings: 1

Ingredients

- ½ cup oats rolled
- ½ cup oat milk or almond
- 1 tbsp almond butter & chia seeds
- ½ tsp Sweet Nature
- 1 tbsp almonds finely chopped

Method

- Put everything that doesn't need to be cooked into an empty glass container and seal it.
- To ensure a uniform mixture, add the liquids and whisk vigorously.
- Close the jar, store it in the fridge, and have it for breakfast the following morning.

Nutritional Facts: Calories: 380 Kcal, Protein: 12 g, Carbs: 27 g, Fats: 26 g

3.6 Dairy Free Scrambled Eggs

Prep Time: 10 Mins, Cook Time: 10 Mins, Servings: 2

Ingredients

- 4 eggs large
- 2 tbsps coconut milk full fat canned
- 1 tbsp coconut oil
- pepper & Salt

Method

- Put everything except the vegetable oil in a bowl and mix it.
- Coconut oil should be melted in a small pan over low heat. When ready, add the eggs and stir.
- Slowly simmer the egg mixture over low heat, stirring it gently with a spatula.
- When the eggs are done to your satisfaction, take them off the fire.
- Include cooked tomato and mushroom slices.

Nutritional Facts: Calories: 150 Kcal, Protein: 13 g, Carbs: 1.5 g, Fats: 11 g

3.7 Low Carb Breakfast Eggs

Prep Time: 05 Mins, Cook Time: 20 Mins, Servings: 4

Ingredients

- 1 cup pumpkin pieces chopped
- 8 eggs
- ¼ cup coconut milk full fat
- 2 tbsps olives chopped & olive oil
- 1 tsp dried oregano & ground cumin

Method

- Melt the fat (olive oil or whatever) in a large skillet over a medium-high flame.
- In a large bowl, mix up everything else, save the pumpkin, using a whisk.
- Gently whisk the egg mixture while it cooks in the frying pan till the eggs are nearly set.
- Stir around the pumpkin dice, then turn off the heat.
- Serve.

Nutritional Facts: Calories: 72 Kcal, Protein: 6 g, Carbs: 0 g, Fats: 5 g

3.8 Pumpkin and Zucchini Frittata

Prep Time: 15 Mins, Cook Time: 15 Mins, Servings: 2

Ingredients

- 6 whisked eggs
- ¼ cup flour/almond meal
- 2 coarsely grated large zucchinis
- 2-inch coarsely grated slice of pumpkin
- ¼ cup each of parsley dried, pitted olives & olive oil

Method

- Turn the oven temperature up to 355°F.
- Butter a pie plate.
- Toss everything together in a bowl and serve.
- Set slightly brown in the oven, which should take around 30 mins.
- Eat with a side of salad.

Nutritional Facts: Calories: 396 Kcal, Protein: 17 g, Carbs: 14 g, Fats: 30 g

3.9 Avocado and Egg Cups

Prep Time: 10 Mins, Cook Time: 15 Mins, Servings: 2

Ingredients

- 4 eggs
- 2 avocados
- 1 tbsp parsley finely chopped
- Salt & pepper

Method

- Prepare a baking dish by lining it with baking paper and heating the oven to 350° F.
- Carefully split the avocados into half and scoop out the pit.
- Spread the avocados out on the baking sheet and cut side up.
- Scoop out some of the avocado flesh using a spoon to create a way for the egg if your avocados are on the small side.
- In each half of an avocado, crack one egg and season with pepper and salt.
- Put in the oven and bake for fifteen to twenty mins, till the egg is done.
- Parsley chives may be used as a garnish.

Nutritional Facts: Calories: 215 Kcal, Protein: 9 g, Carbs: 6 g, Fats: 17 g

3.10 Tomato Omelette

Prep Time: 10 Mins, Cook Time: 05 Mins, Servings: 1

Ingredients

- 3 large eggs
- 1 large chopped ripe tomato
- 1 tbsp goat cheese crumbled
- Salt & pepper
- 1 tbsp butter & olive oil

Method

- Oil or butter should be heated in a pan on a medium-high flame.
- Mix the water, salt, and pepper into the eggs in a bowl. The eggs should be poured into the heated pan. Spread the cheese and chopped tomato on one side of the omelet.
- Fold your omelet to enclose the filling when your eggs are almost set. You should keep frying the eggs until they reach the desired doneness. Enjoy.

Nutritional Facts: Calories: 113 Kcal, Protein: 7 g, Carbs: 21 g, Fats: 5 g

3.11 Breakfast Spinach Omelet

Prep Time: 10 Mins, Cook Time: 20 Mins, Servings: 1-2

Ingredients

- 3 lightly whisked eggs
- 1 large spinach leaves handful baby
- 1 tbsp parsley leaves, finely chopped
- 1 tbsp oil olive
- Salt & pepper

Method

- Olive oil should be heated in a pan over medium heat.
- Salt and pepper the eggs after you've whisked them. Stir the eggs gently till they have the consistency of very wet scrambled eggs.
- Press the spinach, parsley, & goat cheese into the eggs and spread them throughout half of the omelet.
- The omelet should be folded in half after a min. The base should be set after further cooking. Take it off the heat and serve.

Nutritional Facts: Calories: 236 Kcal, Protein: 16 g, Carbs: 3.7 g, Fats: 17 g

3.12 Chia and Oat Porridge

Prep Time: 10 Mins, Cook Time: 15 Mins, Servings: 1

Ingredients

- 4 tbsp oats
- 1 tbsp seeds chia
- ½ cup almond, hemp, or coconut milk & blueberries
- 2 tbsp almonds slivered
- 1 sliced banana

Method

- Combine the oats and water in a small saucepan and simmer on medium.
- To soften the oats, cook for about 10 mins while stirring often.
- Add more water if the ingredients are drying or settling to the base.
- Remove the pan from the heat and whisk in the chia seeds & milk of your choice. Cook 5 mins covered.
- Sprinkle some almonds on top & serve with blueberries & a banana.

Nutritional Facts: Calories: 65 Kcal, Protein: 32 g, Carbs: 85 g, Fats: 14 g

3.13 Easy Turkey Omelet

Prep Time: 05 Mins, Cook Time: 10 Mins, Servings: 2

Ingredients

- 3 lightly whisked eggs
- ½ cup shredded turkey cooked
- 4 chopped sundried tomatoes
- 1 tbsp oil olive
- Salt & pepper

Method

- Olive oil should be heated in a pan over a medium-high flame.
- The eggs should be poured into the pan after being whisked and seasoned.
- Turkey and tomato slices should be pressed into the eggs and spread throughout half of the omelet.
- The omelet should be folded in half after a min. The base should be set after further cooking.
- Take it out of the oven, split it, and serve.

Nutritional Facts: Calories: 54 Kcal, Protein: 49 g, Carbs: 56 g, Fats: 14 g

3.14 Raspberry Chia Pudding

Prep Time: 10 Mins, Cook Time: 20 Mins, Servings: 2

Ingredients

- 1 cup raspberries fresh or frozen
- 1 cup coconut milk
- 3 tbsps seeds chia
- 2 tbsps yogurt plain full fat
- 2 tbsp almonds flaked

Method

- Remove the almonds & chia seeds and combine the other ingredients till smooth.
- Divide the mixture evenly between two bowls and stir with the chia seeds.
- Following 5 mins, give it another good stir before storing it in the fridge for the night.
- Flaked almonds may be added the next morning.

Nutritional Facts: Calories: 312 Kcal, Protein: 10 g, Carbs: 24 g, Fats: 20 g

3.15 Grain Free Hemp Seed Porridge

Prep Time: 05 Mins, Cook Time: 15 Mins, Servings: 1

Ingredients

- 1 cup coconut milk or almond
- ½ cup hemp seeds raw, shelled
- 1 tbsp seeds chia
- 1 tbsp chia seeds ground
- 1 tsp of vanilla

Method

- Put everything in a pot and stir it up.
- Bring to a boil while stirring.
- Reduce the heat to low & cook the porridge, stirring occasionally, for about 2 mins or until it achieves the desired consistency. The longer you let the porridge sit, the thicker it will get.
- Add fruit & more almond milk to your dish of porridge.

Nutritional Facts: Calories: 270 Kcal, Protein: 15 g, Carbs: 37 g, Fats: 17 g

3.16 Quick and Simple Raspberry Bread

Prep Time: 15 Mins, Cook Time: 15 Mins, Servings: 2

Ingredients

- 3 cups almond butter & almond meal
- 2 eggs large
- 1 tsp essence vanilla
- 1 cup raspberries frozen
- ½ cup toasted pecan pieces

Method

- Start by preheating the oven to 375 degrees F. Combine the eggs & almond butter by beating them together.
- Put in the rest besides the raspberries. Combine the raspberries by stirring them in.
- Bake for 40–45 mins, or until the center is cooked, after spooning the batter into a buttered loaf pan.

Nutritional Facts: Calories: 210 Kcal, Protein: 3 g, Carbs: 28 g, Fats: 10 g

3.17 Breakfast Quinoa Porridge

Prep Time: 10 Mins, Cook Time: 10 Mins, Servings: 2

Ingredients

- 1 cup of quinoa
- 2 & ½ cups of water
- 4 cups hemp, almond, coconut milk
- ⅓ cup of berries
- ¼ cup almonds flaked

Method

- For 30 seconds, drain the quinoa in a monetary penalty mesh strainer under running water.
- Rinse the quinoa under cold running water, then add it and the water to a saucepan on the heat. The quinoa should be boiled and lowered to a simmer with the cover off. For about 20 mins, or until all the water is absorbed, cook the quinoa over low heat.
- Cook over low heat, stirring often, until the mixture is thick, and then add the almonds.
- To serve, divide into dishes and sprinkle with almond flakes.

Nutritional Facts: Calories: 219 Kcal, Protein: 7 g, Carbs: 35 g, Fats: 2.8 g

3.18 Hemp Bars

Prep Time: 10 Mins, Cook Time: 15 Mins, Servings: 2

Ingredients

- 1 cup flaxseeds & hemp seeds
- 1 & ½ cups shredded coconut unsweetened
- 2 tbsps seeds sesame
- ½ cup melted coconut butter
- 2 tbsps berries goji

Method

- In a blender, pulse the flaxseeds, hemp seeds, & sesame seeds until they are mostly pulverized, but the texture of the mixture is still coarse.
- Combine all of the ingredients in a bowl and stir to combine.
- Put the mixture in a baking dish and chill it in the fridge to set. Cut the bars into squares after they have set.

Nutritional Facts: Calories: 190 Kcal, Protein: 7 g, Carbs: 24 g, Fats: 9 g

3.19 Plum and Quinoa Porridge

Prep Time: 10 Mins, Cook Time: 15 Mins, Servings: 4

Ingredients

- 1 cup of quinoa
- 2 cup milk coconut
- 4 chopped plums
- 1 cup of water
- 1 tsp essence vanilla

Method

- Run clean water through a sieve set over a bowl to clean the quinoa.
- Put the quinoa, coconut milk, and water into a saucepan and boil over high heat.
- Put it over low heat and let it gently simmer. Combine the plum pieces with the vanilla extract.
- Cook the porridge, stirring often, until it has thickened. There might be a need for extra coconut milk. Serve.

Nutritional Facts: Calories: 70 Kcal, Protein: 2 g, Carbs: 12 g, Fats: 1 g

3.20 Easy Guacamole

Prep Time: 10 Mins, Cook Time: 20 Mins, Servings: 2

Ingredients

- 2 medium diced avocados
- ¼ finely diced red onion
- 2 tbsp finely diced fresh cilantro
- 1 small finely chopped ripe tomato
- 2 tbsps juice lime

Method

- Scoop out the avocado meat & mash it using a fork into a bowl. To this, add the rest of the ingredients and mix them up well.
- Eat as a snack with veggie sticks, or include it in your morning omelet.

Nutritional Facts: Calories: 27 Kcal, Protein: 0.4 g, Carbs: 4 g, Fats: 2 g

3.21 Easy Banana Pancakes

Prep Time: 05 Mins, Cook Time: 20 Mins, Servings: 1

Ingredients

- 2 mashed small bananas
- 2 lightly whisked eggs
- ½ tsp essence of vanilla

Method

- One or two cloves, finely ground. To use in the kitchen: butter, ghee, or coconut oil. Throw everything into a dish and mix it up.
- Melt butter or your preferred fat in a pan and set it over medium heat. When the bottom of the pan is firm, pour in the remaining batter.
- To finish cooking, turn the meat over. To finish, proceed with the remaining batter. Accompany with a side of fruit.

Nutritional Facts: Calories: 78 Kcal, Protein: 2 g, Carbs: 10 g, Fats: 4 g

3.22 Creamy Berry Breakfast Smoothie

Prep Time: 10 Mins, Cook Time: 15 Mins, Servings: 1

Ingredients

- 2 tbsps protein powder whey
- ½ cup berries fresh/frozen
- 1 tbsp oil coconut
- 1 cup of water
- 1 tbsp flaxseed ground

Method

- Blend all the ingredients in a food processor until they are completely combined.

Nutritional Facts: Calories: 281 Kcal, Protein: 4 g, Carbs: 59 g, Fats: 6 g

3.23 Strawberry and Coconut Smoothie

Prep Time: 05 Mins, Cook Time: 05 Mins, Servings: 2

Ingredients

- 1 tbsp oil coconut
- 2 tbsps protein powder whey
- ½ cup strawberries fresh/frozen
- 1 tbsp seeds chia
- 1 tsp butter almond

Method

- Put everything in a blender and whirl it up until it's completely smooth.

Nutritional Facts: Calories: 408 Kcal, Protein: 7 g, Carbs: 48 g, Fats: 22 g

3.24 Grain Free Banana Muffins

Prep Time: 05 Mins, Cook Time: 25 Mins, Servings: 4

Ingredients

- 3 medium bananas, very ripe
- 3 eggs large
- 1 tbsp of honey
- 1 tsp each of tsp soda baking & extract of vanilla
- 1/3 cup flour coconut

Method

- Turn on the oven to 350F. Stir the mashed bananas with a fork to ensure even distribution. Combine the mashed bananas & eggs in a bowl and softly beat the eggs with a fork. Mix in your preferred sugar substitute and vanilla essence.

- Combine baking soda and coconut flour in a big bowl to make a cake. Spoon in the banana concoction and stir to combine. Add chopped chocolate & pecans after the mixture has been blended.

- Spoon batter into prepared muffin cups and bake for 30 mins, till a toothpick inserted in the center comes out clean.

Nutritional Facts: Calories: 332 Kcal, Protein: 5 g, Carbs: 51 g, Fats: 12 g

3.25 Low-carb Coconut Blueberry Pancakes

Prep Time: 05 Mins, Cook Time: 20 Mins, Servings: 4

Ingredients

- 4 large eggs
- 1 cup each of flour coconut & coconut milk
- 2 tbsps butter coconut
- handful of blueberries, fresh
- 1 tsp of baking soda

Method

- In a dish, vigorously combine the eggs. Mix in everything else but the coconut flour & the blueberries.

- Blueberries should be added after the coconut flour has been mixed in. Slowly add the mixture, a quarter cup, to a pan heated over medium.

- Flip after 3–4 mins of cooking time and continue cooking the other side. Accompany with coconut cream and fresh fruit.

Nutritional Facts: Calories: 261 Kcal, Protein: 11 g, Carbs: 17 g, Fats: 17 g

3.26 Berry Delicious - A Great Low-Carb, High-Protein Breakfast
Prep Time: 05 Mins, Cook Time: 25 Mins, Servings: 1

Ingredients

- 1 cup berries mixed
- 1 tbsp mixed berries extra
- 1 tbsp yogurt, plain unsweetened
- 1 tbsp Powder Protein

Method

- Spread protein powder over fruit in a serving dish.
- Blend the remaining berries with the yogurt and serve it over top.
- You may top the yogurt with some LSA and chopped nuts if you'd like.

Nutritional Facts: Calories: 100 Kcal, Protein: 15 g, Carbs: 7 g, Fats: 1 g

3.27 Quinoa Strawberry High Protein Porridge
Prep Time: 10 Mins, Cook Time: 15 Mins, Servings: 2

Ingredients

- 1 & ½ cups milk almond
- ½ cup of quinoa
- 1 tbsp seeds chia
- 1 tbsp each of Powder Protein & seeds of hemp
- ½ cup fresh strawberries chopped

Method

- Milk should be heated and brought to a boil in a small saucepan. Turn the heat down to a low simmer, then add the hemp, quinoa, & chia seeds. For around 15 mins, with the lid on, quinoa should simmer and thicken. Occasionally, during cooking, you will have to stir the contents of the pot.
- Remove from the fire and stir in the rest of the ingredients. Wait 5 mins with the cover on, then transfer to serving dishes.

Nutritional Facts: Calories: 90 Kcal, Protein: 10 g, Carbs: 23 g, Fats: 0.5 g

3.28 Grain-Free Pecan Muesli

Prep Time: 05 Mins, Cook Time: 20 Mins, Servings: 4

Ingredients

- 1 cup pecan halves toasted
- 1/3 cup pumpkin seeds unsalted shelled
- ½ cup each of coconut flakes unsweetened, dried cloves & cinnamon
- 2 finely diced dried dates
- 3 tbsps seeds hemp

Method

- Combine everything in a glass container and shake thoroughly before using. Serve with milk of your choice in the morning.

Nutritional Facts: Calories: 267 Kcal, Protein: 7 g, Carbs: 4 g, Fats: 23 g

3.29 Coffee Cacao Porridge

Prep Time: 10 Mins, Cook Time: 20 Mins, Servings: 1

Ingredients

- ½ cup oats rolled
- 1 tbsp powdered cacao
- ¾ cup almond milk & hemp
- ¼ cup each of roasted pecans chopped & coffee brewed
- 1 tsp extract of vanilla

Method

- Cook everything in a small saucepan over a medium-low flame except the pecans and vanilla. If the mix gets too thick, add more milk and keep stirring.
- To the desired tenderness, cook the oats.
- Mix in the vanilla extract and chopped pecans, and savor.

Nutritional Facts: Calories: 174 Kcal, Protein: 7 g, Carbs: 22 g, Fats: 7 g

3.30 Grain Free Coconut Granola

Prep Time: 05 Mins, Cook Time: 20 Mins, Servings: 3

Ingredients

- 2 cups sugar-free coconut chips
- ½ cup of chopped almonds & pecans
- ¼ cup each of seeds sunflower, honey & coconut oil
- 1 tsp ground cinnamon & chia seeds

- ½ tsp cloves ground

Method

- Start by preheating the oven to 375°F.
- In a small saucepan, combine the coconut oil and honey and heat until the honey has melted.
- Throw the rest into a big dish and stir it up. Add the honey mixture to the other ingredients and mix well.
- Bake for 15–20 mins, until mixture is gently browned, on a baking sheet that has been lined or oiled.
- Top with yogurt or your preferred milk, and serve. You may nibble on this grain-free coconut granola on its own.

Nutritional Facts: Calories: 180 Kcal, Protein: 4 g, Carbs: 11 g, Fats: 14 g

3.31 Scrambled Eggs with Sweet Potato
Prep Time: 10 Mins, Cook Time: 20 Mins, Servings: 4

Ingredients

- 1 large potato sweet
- 8 large eggs
- ¼ cup coconut milk canned full fat & ghee or olive oil
- 2 tbsps finely chopped fresh parsley
- 1 tsp cumin ground & oregano dried

Method

- Melt the ghee or olive oil over medium heat in a large skillet.
- Whisk together everything else except the sweet potato in a large bowl.
- Gently whisk the egg mixture in the frying pan until the eggs become nearly set.
- Stir in the cubed sweet potato and turn off the heat.
- Serve.

Nutritional Facts: Calories: 171 Kcal, Protein: 22 g, Carbs: 28 g, Fats: 19 g

3.32 Grain Free Egg Muffins
Prep Time: 15 Mins, Cook Time: 15 Mins, Servings: 3

Ingredients

- 6 whisked large eggs
- ¼ finely diced red pepper & red onion
- 3 oz finely chopped pastured bacon
- 1 handful finely chopped parsley

- 1 tbsp of pesto

Method

- Turn oven temperature up to 350°F.

- The eggs and pesto should be whisked together until smooth. Add the rest of the ingredients and stir.

- The mixture should be poured into oiled muffin cups and baked for about 20 mins. The amount of time needed to bake muffins varies depending on their size.

Nutritional Facts: Calories: 259 Kcal, Protein: 20 g, Carbs: 11 g, Fats: 14 g

3.33 Oven Baked Omelette

Prep Time: 15 Mins, Cook Time: 15 Mins, Servings: 4

Ingredients

- 8 eggs

- 1 cup red pepper & chopped pumpkin

- ¼ cup sliced red onion, olives & olive oil

- 1/3 cup of coconut milk full-fat

- 1 tsp oregano dried

Method

- Set oven temperature to 400°F.

- Over a medium-high flame, sauté the pumpkin & onion in a drizzle of olive oil until aromatic and softened slightly. Toss in some pepper. Keep cooking for a few more mins.

- Combine the eggs and milk in a big bowl and mix.

- Cover everything in a big baking dish with the egg mixture. Put in the oven and bake for about thirty mins.

- Serve.

Nutritional Facts: Calories: 323 Kcal, Protein: 22 g, Carbs: 19 g, Fats: 17 g

3.34 Apple and cinnamon pancakes

Prep Time: 10 Mins, Cook Time: 15 Mins, Servings: 1

Ingredients

- 2 whisked eggs

- 2 medium finely diced apple & mashed bananas

- 2 tbsps butter peanut

- 1 tsp ground cinnamon

- 1 tbsp oil coconut

Method

- Combine the mashed bananas & eggs in a bowl. Put in the rest of the ingredients except the coconut oil.

- Pancakes are best when fried in coconut oil over a medium-high flame on both sides.

- They will stay together better if they are smaller than traditional pancakes. Use it as a dessert or a morning meal.

Nutritional Facts: Calories: 135 Kcal, Protein: 4 g, Carbs: 21 g, Fats: 4 g

3.35 Pesto Frittata
Prep Time: 05 Mins, Cook Time: 25 Mins, Servings: 4

Ingredients

- 8 lightly whisked eggs

- ½ cup sliced pitted olives & mushrooms sliced

- 1 tbsp ghee or pastured butter

- ½ sliced red pepper

- 3 tbsps of pesto

Method

- Butter should be heated in a pan with an oven-safe handle. When the pan is heated, toss in the mushrooms & peppers.

- Slowly heat until tender. Turn the oven temperature up to 370 degrees Fahrenheit. Mix in the pesto & olives gently.

- Carefully add the egg mixture to the pan and distribute it evenly. Goat cheese should be added.

- The eggs are done when they separate from the pan during cooking. Cook within the oven once the top has set, about 10 mins. Accompany with a side of salad or steaming greens.

Nutritional Facts: Calories: 350 Kcal, Protein: 19 g, Carbs: 22 g, Fats: 19 g

3.36 Stuffed Peppers
Prep Time: 5 Mins, Cook Time: 25 Mins, Servings: 4

Ingredients

- 4 core & seeds removed bell peppers

- 8 beaten eggs

- 1 cup halved cherry tomatoes & fresh mushrooms diced

- 1 diced large carrot & red onion

- 1 tbsp dried oregano & olive oil

Method

- Turn the oven temperature up to 375 degrees Fahrenheit.
- The onion should be softened in olive oil while sautéing. Continue cooking by adding the mushrooms, tomatoes, and carrots to the pan.
- Prepare with salt, pepper, & oregano. Stuff the peppers with the mixture, then divide the beaten egg mixture among the 4 peppers.
- Spread the peppers out on a baking sheet that has been oiled and bake them for about 30 mins.

Nutritional Facts: Calories: 140 Kcal, Protein: 7 g, Carbs: 23 g, Fats: 3 g

3.37 Grain Free Banana and Pecan Bread

Prep Time: 10 Mins, Cook Time: 20 Mins, Servings: 2

Ingredients

- ½ cup of flour almond & coconut
- ½ cup coconut oil, butter or melted ghee
- 4 whisked eggs & mashed bananas
- 1 tsp ground cinnamon & baking soda
- ½ cup mashed pumpkin & pecans chopped toasted

Method

- Prepare a 350°F oven. Whisk together the flour, spices, & baking soda.
- Whisk together everything else but the pecans. Add the liquid to the dry ingredients & mix well. The pecans should be mixed in at this point.
- Bake the batter for forty-five mins, till a toothpick inserted in the center comes out clean.

Nutritional Facts: Calories: 350 Kcal, Protein: 5 g, Carbs: 46 g, Fats: 19 g

3.38 Roasted Sweet Potato Omelets

Prep Time: 10 Mins, Cook Time: 10 Mins, Servings: 3

Ingredients

- 1 & ½ cups sweet potato diced
- ½ sliced red onion
- 1 tsp Coconut oil
- 6 whisked eggs
- 1 handful chopped fresh parsley

Method

- Put the cut onion & sweet potato on an oiled baking sheet. Add some dried oregano and your favorite oil and sprinkle with it.

- Put in the oven and cook until tender and golden brown. Warm the oil of choice for cooking in a skillet over medium heat. Put everything into the pan except the eggs.

- Pour the beaten eggs over the ingredients and spread them so they're uniformly coated. The egg should be cooked for around 5 mins. The cooking time will be cut in half if you cover the pan.

Nutritional Facts: Calories: 120 Kcal, Protein: 1 g, Carbs: 25 g, Fats: 2 g

3.39 Breakfast Muffins
Prep Time: 10 Mins, Cook Time: 20 Mins, Servings: 3

Ingredients

- 8 large eggs
- 1 diced red bell pepper
- ¼ cup pitted olives sliced
- 2 finely diced brown onion & button mushrooms
- 1 tsp oregano dried

Method

- Prepare a 350°F oven.
- Scramble the eggs in a bowl. Add the other ingredients and mix well.
- The mixture may be baked in oiled or prepared muffin pans for about 20 mins.

Nutritional Facts: Calories: 209 Kcal, Protein: 8 g, Carbs: 41 g, Fats: 2 g

3.40 Grain Free Sweet Potato Bread
Prep Time: 05 Mins, Cook Time: 15 Mins, Servings: 3

Ingredients

- 1 medium cooked & mashed sweet potato
- 3 eggs large
- ½ cup each of flour coconut & milk almond
- 3 tsp fresh chives finely chopped & bicarb soda
- 1 tsp lemon juice, fresh & dried oregano

Method

- Prepare a 350°F oven. In a large bowl, thoroughly mix all of the ingredients.
- Mix well by beating for about 2 mins with electric beaters.
- Put the batter into a oiled and floured loaf pan and bake for about 20 mins. Time in the oven and baking dish selection will affect the final result.

Nutritional Facts: Calories: 67 Kcal, Protein: 2 g, Carbs: 12 g, Fats: 0.8 g

3.41 Grain Free Granola

Prep Time: 10 Mins, Cook Time: 20 Mins, Servings: 2

Ingredients

- 2 cups raw almonds
- 1 cup each of coconut flakes, pecan halves & raw cashews
- 2 whites egg
- 2 tsps ground cinnamon, honey & coconut oil melted
- ½ tsp ground cloves & cardamom

Method

- Reduce the nuts' size by chopping or briefly processing them using a food processor.
- At start, turn on the oven to 350 degrees Fahrenheit. Foam up the egg whites by beating them with a mixture of honey & spices.
- Blend in the rest of the ingredients. Bake the mixture for about 20 mins, until golden brown, after spreading it out on a oiled and lined baking pan. The mixture will need to be stirred a few times during baking.

Nutritional Facts: Calories: 170 Kcal, Protein: 5 g, Carbs: 10 g, Fats: 13 g

3.42 Grain-Free Porridge

Prep Time: 10 Mins, Cook Time: 20 Mins, Servings: 1

Ingredients

- 2 tbsps shredded coconut unsweetened
- 1 tbsp sunflower seeds raw
- 1 tbsp chia seeds & linseeds flaxseeds
- 2 tbsps hazelnuts raw
- ¼ cup of almond milk

Method

- Combine everything in a food processor except the liquids and blend until powdery.
- It's preferable to not entirely powder it but instead leave some bigger lumps. To serve, transfer the porridge mixture to a bowl.
- Add the heated water to the dry ingredients and whisk to combine. Wait 5-10 mins for the mixture to thicken, then whisk it a couple more times. Enjoy with a glass of milk on top.

Nutritional Facts: Calories: 104 Kcal, Protein: 16 g, Carbs: 24 g, Fats: 4 g

3.43 Grain-Free Strawberry Muffins

Prep Time: 15 Mins, Cook Time: 15 Mins, Servings: 2

Ingredients

- 1 cup meal almond
- 6 tbsps flour arrowroot
- 1 lightly whisked large egg
- ¼ cup honey & coconut oil melted
- ½ cup strawberries chopped fresh

Method

- Prepare a 350-degree Fahrenheit oven. In a large bowl, mix the arrowroot & almond meal.
- Mix everything with a spoon except the chopped strawberries.
- Combine with strawberry pieces. Put the batter into muffin cups that have been oiled or lined, then bake for twenty to twenty-five mins, till a toothpick inserted in the center comes out clean.

Nutritional Facts: Calories: 153 Kcal, Protein: 7 g, Carbs: 21 g, Fats: 4 g

3.44 Grain Free Carrot and Ginger Muffins

Prep Time: 10 Mins, Cook Time: 20 Mins, Servings: 12

Ingredients

- 2 cups flour almond
- 1 tsp each of soda baking, powdered ginger & ground cloves
- ½ cup shredded coconut unsweetened & melted ghee
- 1 & ½ cups grated carrot & toasted pecans
- 3 eggs, whisked

Method

- Prepare a 350F oven.
- Mix the ginger, cloves, baking soda, almond flour, and coconut in a big bowl.
- Eggs, ghee/oil, and Nature Sweet should be mixed in a smaller bowl. Combine the liquids with the dry ones and mix well. Mix in the chopped carrot and nuts.
- Fill muffin pans with the batter and bake for approximately twenty to twenty-five mins.

Nutritional Facts: Calories: 133 Kcal, Protein: 1 g, Carbs: 14 g, Fats: 2.9 g

3.45 Mushroom and Onion Omelet

Prep Time: 15 Mins, Cook Time: 10 Mins, Servings: 4

Ingredients

- ½ chopped red onion & red seeded capsicum
- 5 button sliced mushrooms.
- 1 roughly grated carrot
- 2 tbsps each of oil olive, ricotta cheese & finely chopped fresh parsley.
- 6 eggs

Method

- Fry the onion, pepper, and mushrooms in a tbsp of olive oil till tender.
- Put the veggies in a bowl and season with salt and pepper, as well as the parsley and carrot.
- In a large container, combine the eggs, egg whites, and water and whisk.
- Reheat the pan and add the olive oil, one tsp at a time. Tilt the pan to properly distribute the egg mixture after pouring half of it.
- When the omelet's sides are set, flip it over with a spatula so the raw egg can flow beneath. Sprinkle half the veggie mixture and half the cheese on top and cook for an additional min.
- To fold the omelet over the filling, gently raise one side with a spatula. Split the omelet in two and serve.
- Repeat the previous steps to make a second omelet and divide it in half. Salad on the side, please.

Nutritional Facts: Calories: 200 Kcal, Protein: 14 g, Carbs: 10 g, Fats: 10 g

3.46 Pumpkin and Olive Frittata

Prep Time: 5 Mins, Cook Time: 25 Mins, Servings: 2

Ingredients

- 6 whisked eggs
- ¼ cup each of melted ghee or olive oil & flour/almond meal
- 2 cups grated pumpkin coarsely
- 1 small finely diced brown onion
- ¼ cup finely chopped red pepper & pitted olives

Method

- Set the temperature to 355 degrees Fahrenheit.
- Prepare a oiled baking dish.
- Toss everything together in a bowl and serve.
- Set slightly brown in the oven, which should take around 30 mins.

- Salad on the side, please.

Nutritional Facts: Calories: 203 Kcal, Protein: 13 g, Carbs: 7 g, Fats: 10 g

3.47 Pumpkin Pancakes

Prep Time: 15 Mins, Cook Time: 15 Mins, Servings: 2

Ingredients

- 4 whisked eggs
- ½ cup cooked pumpkin mashed
- 1 tsp vanilla extract & cinnamon
- ¼ tsp each of soda baking & cloves ground
- 1 tbsp coconut oil or melted ghee

Method

- Eggs, pumpkin, & ghee (or oil) should be whisked together.
- Toss in the rest of the ingredients and mix well with a whisk.
- Pancakes are best when cooked in a skillet with extra ghee or oil over medium heat. When bubbles form on the top of the pancakes, it's time to flip them.
- Accompany with coconut cream and fresh fruit.

Nutritional Facts: Calories: 130 Kcal, Protein: 4 g, Carbs: 21 g, Fats: 3 g

Chapter 4: Wholesome Lunches and Snacks

Here are some lunch and snack recipes to purify your liver to regain health and energy.

4.1 Chicken Patties

Prep Time: 05 Mins, Cook Time: 25 Mins, Servings: 4

Ingredients

- 1 lb chicken, ground
- 2 tbsps fresh cilantro finely chopped
- 1 finely grated large carrot
- 1 tsp oregano, dried
- ½ tsp of salt

Method

- Turn the oven temperature up to 360 degrees. Put everything in a bowl and mix it up with your hands until it's fully combined.
- Make burgers out of the mixture and set them on a baking sheet. Brown and fully cook in the oven, usually around 25 mins.

Nutritional Facts: Calories: 244 Kcal, Protein: 13 g, Carbs: 11 g, Fats: 17 g

4.2 Roasted Turkey Drumsticks

Prep Time: 10 Mins, Cook Time: 20 Mins, Servings: 2

Ingredients

- 2 drumsticks turkey
- ½ tsp of salt
- 1 tbsp ghee pastured
- 1 tbsp cumin, ground
- ¼ tsp pepper, cayenne

Method

- Turn the oven temperature up to 360 degrees.
- Use your hands to massage the drumsticks with the cumin, salt, and cayenne.
- Coat the drumsticks with the ghee or butter that has been melted.
- Bake the drumsticks for 20 mins, till fully done, on a prepared baking sheet. The length of time needed to cook drumsticks varies with their size. Cover them with aluminum foil if they're browning too quickly.

Nutritional Facts: Calories: 189 Kcal, Protein: 31 g, Carbs: 0 g, Fats: 6.4 g

4.3 Easy Lemon Baked Salmon

Prep Time: 10 Mins, Cook Time: 15 Mins, Servings: 2

Ingredients

- 2 fresh fillets of salmon
- ¼ cup oil olive
- 2 tbsps lemon, fresh juice
- 1 tsp cumin, ground
- 2 tbsps fresh dill, finely chopped

Method

- Put everything except the salmon in a glass dish and stir until combined. Ensure the salmon fillets are well submerged in the marinade before adding them to the bowl.
- Wrap the bowl and chill for at least two hours in the fridge.
- For about 15 mins in an oven set to 400°F, or until desired doneness, bake the salmon.
- Eat with a side of salad.

Nutritional Facts: Calories: 196 Kcal, Protein: 21 g, Carbs: 3 g, Fats: 11 g

4.4 Simple Baked Salmon

Prep Time: 10 Mins, Cook Time: 20 Mins, Servings: 4

Ingredients

- 30 oz salmon steaks fresh
- 1 thinly sliced lemon
- 1 tbsp oil olive
- 1 tsp lemon zest freshly grated
- 1 tbsp thyme leaves fresh/dried

Method

- Turn the oven on to 390 degrees F.
- Arrange the salmon fillets skin-side down on a baking sheet. Garnish the fish with lemon wedges.
- Sprinkle the remaining ingredients over the fish.
- Put it in the oven & bake for about 20 mins or until it reaches the desired doneness. The thickness of the salmon slices will determine this.
- Pair with some roasted veggies or a salad.

Nutritional Facts: Calories: 196 Kcal, Protein: 20.8 g, Carbs: 12 g, Fats: 4 g

4.5 Grilled Tuna Steaks

Prep Time: 05 Mins, Cook Time: 05 Mins, Servings: 2

Ingredients

- 2 steaks tuna
- 2 tbsp olive oil or ghee
- 2 garlic cloves crushed
- 1 lime Juice & zest
- 1 sliced avocado

Method

- In a glass dish, thoroughly combine everything, excluding the tuna & avocado. Put the tuna steaks inside the bowl & use your hands to coat them with the marinade. To chill for 4 hours, cover the bowl.
- The steaks should be grilled for 5 mins each side over medium to high heat or until they reach the desired doneness. Avocados and salad should accompany the steaks.

Nutritional Facts: Calories: 184 Kcal, Protein: 41 g, Carbs: 0 g, Fats: 0.8 g

4.6 Garlic Spicy Chicken

Prep Time: 10 Mins, Cook Time: 20 Mins, Servings: 4

Ingredients

- 3 lbs drumsticks chicken
- 1 tbsp garlic powder, smoked paprika & ground cumin
- ½ tsp chili powder & salt
- ¼ cup of olive oil

Method

- Put everything in a big dish except the chicken. Toss in chicken drumsticks, then use your hands to thoroughly cover them in the mixture.
- To ensure the chicken is cooked, grill it for 20 mins on all sides over a medium-high flame.
- Eat with a side of salad.

Nutritional Facts: Calories: 265 Kcal, Protein: 27 g, Carbs: 23 g, Fats: 6 g

4.7 Rosemary Pork Chops

Prep Time: 10 Mins, Cook Time: 20 Mins, Servings: 3

Ingredients

- 6 pork chops thin, boneless
- 1 tbsp oil olive
- 1 tbsp ghee or pastured butter
- 1 tbsp of finely chopped rosemary leaves fresh
- Salt & pepper

Method

- Put the oil and butter in a pan and heat it over moderate. Add pepper and salt to the pork chops before cooking. After heating the pan, add the pork chops and some rosemary.
- Ensure all sides of the chops are cooked through and browned for maximum flavor.
- Serve.

Nutritional Facts: Calories: 590 Kcal, Protein: 31 g, Carbs: 47 g, Fats: 31 g

4.8 Grain-Free Lamb Patties

Prep Time: 10 Mins, Cook Time: 20 Mins, Servings: 3

Ingredients

- 1 lb lamb ground
- 1 handful finely chopped fresh parsley
- ½ finely grated brown onion
- 2 tbsps fresh rosemary finely chopped
- 2 finely diced cloves garlic

Method

- Prepare a 350°F oven.
- In a big bowl, thoroughly combine all ingredients using your hands.
- Make about 8 patties from the mixture and bake for around 25 mins, till done.

Nutritional Facts: Calories: 250 Kcal, Protein: 20 g, Carbs: 0 g, Fats: 18 g

4.9 Greek Lamb Meatballs

Prep Time: 10 Mins, Cook Time: 20 Mins, Servings: 4

Ingredients

- 1 & ½ lbs of ground lamb
- 1 lightly whisked egg
- 2 minced cloves garlic

- 1 tbsp dried oregano & rosemary
- ¼ cup of diced fresh parsley & fetta cheese

Method

- Start by preheating the oven to 375 degrees F.
- Put everything in a big bowl and mix it. Combine everything by hand and thoroughly mix it.
- Roll the meat into balls and place them in a single layer on an oiled or lined baking sheet.
- Put in the oven and bake for about 20 mins or until done.

Nutritional Facts: Calories: 73 Kcal, Protein: 5 g, Carbs: 1.5 g, Fats: 5 g

4.10 Gluten-Free and Dairy-Free Zucchini Slice

Prep Time: 05 Mins, Cook Time: 25 Mins, Servings: 4

Ingredients

- 6 whisked eggs
- ¼ cup olive oil & flour coconut
- 2 coarsely grated pumpkin & large zucchinis
- 1 small brown onion, finely diced
- ¼ cup chopped pitted olives, sun-dried tomatoes & dried oregano

Method

- Turn the oven temperature up to 355°F.
- Butter a pie plate.
- Toss everything together in a bowl and serve.
- Set & slightly brown in the oven, which should take around 30 mins.
- Eat with a side of salad.

Nutritional Facts: Calories: 157 Kcal, Protein: 9 g, Carbs: 18 g, Fats: 3 g

4.11 Salmon Patties

Prep Time: 10 Mins, Cook Time: 20 Mins, Servings: 3

Ingredients

- 2 cans salmon, drained
- 1 sweet large potato & finely diced red onion
- 2/3 cup meal almond
- 2 tbsps parsley finely chopped & lemon juice
- 2 large eggs

Method

- Put everything in a big bowl and mix it up with your hands. Add a little water or additional lemon juice if the mixture seems too dry to work. Add an extra almond meal if the mixture is too moist. The sweetness of the final product will be affected by the amount of moisture in the sweet potato.

- Make burgers out of the mixture. They turn out great, whether baked on a prepared baking sheet or fried in olive, ghee, or coconut oil.

- Prepare at 355°F for 20 mins.

- Eat with a side of salad.

Nutritional Facts: Calories: 422 Kcal, Protein: 31 g, Carbs: 20 g, Fats: 23 g

4.12 Low FODMAP Tuna Salad

Prep Time: 10 Mins, Cook Time: 20 Mins, Servings: 3

Ingredients

- 1 handful leaves arugula & coarsely grated zucchini

- ½ cup of cherry tomatoes & Lebanese cucumber

- ½ tsp oregano dried

- 6 oz drained tuna canned

- 2 tbsps oil olive & lemon juice

Method

- Combine the salad's components carefully. Drizzle using lemon juice & olive oil.

Nutritional Facts: Calories: 279 Kcal, Protein: 18 g, Carbs: 2 g, Fats: 22 g

4.13 Tender Thyme Lamb Cutlets

Prep Time: 15 Mins, Cook Time: 15 Mins, Servings: 4

Ingredients

- 12 cutlets lamb

- 2 tbsps thyme dried

- 4 tbsps lemon juice fresh

- 4 tbsps oil olive

- Salt & pepper

Method

- Get a glass dish and toss the cutlets in it. Use your hands to evenly coat each cutlet with the olive oil and lemon juice. Put the lid on the bowl and let it chill in the fridge all night.

- Season the cutlets using thyme, salt, & pepper, then grill them. Two to three mins each side should do it.

- Accompany with steamed and roasted veggies.

Nutritional Facts: Calories: 210 Kcal, Protein: 5 g, Carbs: 26 g, Fats: 8 g

4.14 Coconut Seafood Curry

Prep Time: 10 Mins, Cook Time: 5 Mins, Servings: 2

Ingredients

- 1 lb fish white flesh
- 1 can of coconut milk full fat
- 2 cups fish stock, large carrots, brown onion, diced pumpkin, chopped zucchini
- 2 tbsps of curry powder, pepper & Salt
- 1 tsp garam masala, ginger freshly grated & crushed garlic

Method

- Cook the fish separately and add it to the other ingredients in a big saucepan over medium heat. Bring to a boil, reduce heat, and simmer until carrots are tender for about 10 mins.
- The fish should be cooked for about 5 mins over low heat until it easily breaks down the flakes.
- Serve.

Nutritional Facts: Calories: 200 Kcal, Protein: 22 g, Carbs: 7 g, Fats: 8 g

4.15 Tender Grilled Baby Octopus

Prep Time: 10 Mins, Cook Time: 05 Mins, Servings: 4

Ingredients

- 2 lbs octopus baby
- ½ cup of olive oil
- 1 tsp lemon freshly grated, lime zest & lime juice
- 2 cloves crushed garlic
- ½ tsp of salt

Method

- Baby octopus needs a good bath and a trim.
- Bring five cups of warm water to a boil in a big saucepan. Remove the saucepan from the heat and add the octopuses. After a min, remove them from the heat, drain them, and refresh them in cool water.
- In a glass bowl, combine the remaining ingredients. Toss in the octopuses and cover them well. Put the bowl in the fridge and let it sit for about 6 hours covered.
- Turn on a grill's heat to medium. Cook the octopus on the grill for around 5 mins.
- Eat with a side of salad.

Nutritional Facts: Calories: 470 Kcal, Protein: 14 g, Carbs: 0 g, Fats: 39 g

4.16 Tuna Steaks with Avocado

Prep Time: 15 Mins, Cook Time: 15 Mins, Servings: 1

Ingredients

- 1 steak tuna
- 2 tbsps ghee or olive oil
- 1 minced clove garlic
- 2 tbsps juice lime

Method

- Combine the oil, garlic, and lime juice in a glass bowl. Place the tuna steak into the marinade and turn to coat it evenly. Cover the bowl inside the refrigerator for at least two hours.
- Tuna is best when grilled over a medium fire.
- To serve, dish the tuna & salad, then dress the salad with the lime juice & olive oil.

Nutritional Facts: Calories: 384 Kcal, Protein: 45 g, Carbs: 17 g, Fats: 2.1 g

4.17 Chicken and Basil Stir Fry

Prep Time: 10 Mins, Cook Time: 20 Mins, Servings: 4

Ingredients

- 1lb chicken, ground
- 1 sliced red pepper capsicum
- 4 tbsps of olive oil, fish sauce & fresh lime juice
- 1 tbsp tamari
- 1 handful of large fresh torn basil leaves

Method

- A big skillet should be heated with the olive oil.
- Stir-frying the chicken for a few minutes will ensure it is well done.
- Toss in some pepper.
- Add the other ingredients and continue to stir-fry for a few mins.
- Remove the mixture from the heat and add the basil leaves.
- Serve.

Nutritional Facts: Calories: 515 Kcal, Protein: 22 g, Carbs: 70 g, Fats: 15 g

4.18 Homemade Steak Rub

Prep Time: 05 Mins, Cook Time: 15 Mins, Servings: 3

Ingredients

- ¼ cup black pepper ground
- 2 tbsps lightly crushed cumin seeds
- ¼ cup powder onion
- 2 tbsps powder garlic
- 2 tbsps of salt

Method

- Combine everything in a bowl and store in an airtight container. Use the rub on steak, lamb chops, or any other cut of meat before cooking.

Nutritional Facts: Calories: 12 Kcal, Protein: 0.6 g, Carbs: 2.2 g, Fats: 0.5 g

4.19 Vegan Creamy Sweet Potato Curry

Prep Time: 10 Mins, Cook Time: 10 Mins, Servings: 4

Ingredients

- 1 tbsp oil olive
- 1 chopped brown small onion, chopped fresh spinach & sweet potatoes, orange
- 1 sliced red pepper capsicum
- 1 cup vegetable stock, curry paste & canned chickpeas
- 1 can of coconut milk full fat

Method

- Oil should be heated in a big saucepan.
- Add it to the pan to soften the onion and cook for a few minutes.
- Put in the sweet potato and mix it up.
- Then, after 3 mins, add the curry paste and whisk it in thoroughly.
- Put in the remaining components.
- For about 20 mins, simmer the mixture occasionally until the potato is very soft.
- Toss with rice or quinoa and serve.

Nutritional Facts: Calories: 440 Kcal, Protein: 12 g, Carbs: 31 g, Fats: 33 g

4.20 Ground Turkey Patties

Prep Time: 05 Mins, Cook Time: 25 Mins, Servings: 4

Ingredient

- 1 lb turkey, ground
- 2 tbsps fresh parsley, finely chopped
- ½ cup fresh pumpkin, finely grated
- 1 tsp Italian herb dried & finely chopped garlic cloves
- ½ tsp of salt

Method

- Ensure your oven is at a temperature of at least 360 degrees Fahrenheit.
- Put everything in a bowl and mix it up with your hands until it's fully combined.
- Make burgers out of the mixture and set them on a baking sheet. Brown and fully cook in the oven, usually around 25 mins. Eat with a side of salad.

Nutritional Facts: Calories: 847 Kcal, Protein: 88 g, Carbs: 0 g, Fats: 55 g

4.21 Salmon Citrus Salad

Prep Time: 10 Mins, Cook Time: 10 Mins, Servings: 2

Ingredients

- 1 freshly cooked salmon fillet, flaked
- 1 peeled and sliced medium avocado, orange, stalk celery & red onion
- ½ cup sliced cherry tomatoes
- ¼ cup olive oil & lime juice
- Salt & pepper

Method

- Throw everything into a dish and call it a salad. Toss with the lime juice & olive oil.

Nutritional Facts: Calories: 334 Kcal, Protein: 27 g, Carbs: 22 g, Fats: 16 g

4.22 Pesto Frittata

Prep Time: 10 Mins, Cook Time: 15 Mins, Servings: 4

Ingredients

- 8 lightly whisked eggs
- ½ cup sliced pitted olives & mushrooms
- 1 tbsp ghee or pastured butter
- ½ sliced capsicum red pepper
- 3 tbsps of pesto

Method

- Butter should be heated in a pan with an oven-safe handle. Mix in the mushrooms & peppers once the pan is heated. Slow cooking to tenderize. Set the oven temperature to 370 degrees Fahrenheit.

- Mix in the pesto and olives gently. Carefully add the egg mixture to the pan and distribute it evenly. Blend with some goat cheese. The eggs are done when they separate from the pan during cooking. Throw the dish in the oven and let it bake until the top is set. Accompany with a side of salad or steaming greens.

Nutritional Facts: Calories: 300 Kcal, Protein: 21 g, Carbs: 1.4 g, Fats: 23.4 g

4.23 Oregano Grilled Lamb Chops
Prep Time: 10 Mins, Cook Time: 05 Mins, Servings: 2

Ingredients

- 6 chops lamb
- 1 tsp oregano dried
- ¼ cup of lemon juice & lemon zest
- 1 tsp salt & black pepper
- ¼ cup oil olive

Method

- Prepare a glass dish for the lamb chops. Rub the remaining seasonings into the lamb chops with your hands after thoroughly mixing all the ingredients.

- Put the bowl, sealed, in the freezer for at least two hours. Prepare the lamb chops by grilling them for about 5 mins each side. Eat with a side of salad or some steamed greens.

Nutritional Facts: Calories: 220 Kcal, Protein: 29 g, Carbs: 1.1 g, Fats: 11 g

4.24 Spanish Pork Chops
Prep Time: 05 Mins, Cook Time: 25 Mins, Servings: 2

Ingredients

- 2 pork chops
- 2 peeled & chopped small parsnips, large carrot, orange & red pepper
- 1 tsp of ground coriander & cumin
- Salt & pepper
- 1 tbsp of ghee

Method

- Set the oven temperature to 375 degrees Fahrenheit. Spread all the veggies on a baking sheet and sprinkle with ½ of the oil or ghee.

- Use salt and pepper to taste. For around 25 mins, roast the veggies and orange in the oven. Season the pork chops with salt and pepper while you're waiting.

- Lightly brown the chops on all sides in the remaining ghee or oil in a hot pan. Chops, veggies, and a tray should be transferred to the table.
- Chops should be cooked thoroughly before serving, so put them back in the oven. Serve.

Nutritional Facts: Calories: 640 Kcal, Protein: 43 g, Carbs: 43 g, Fats: 37 g

4.25 Hemp Bars

Prep Time: 10 Mins, Cook Time: 20 Mins, Servings: 2

Ingredients

- 1 cup flaxseeds & hemp seeds
- 1 & ½ cups shredded coconut unsweetened
- 2 tbsps seeds sesame
- ½ cup melted coconut butter
- 2 tbsps berries goji

Method

- In a food processor, pulse flaxseeds, hemp seeds, & sesame seeds until they are mostly pulverized, but the texture of the mixture is still coarse.
- Put everything in a bowl and stir until combined.
- In a baking dish, press the mix and chill until stiff. When ready, cut the bars into desired sizes.

Nutritional Facts: Calories: 190 Kcal, Protein: 7 g, Carbs: 24 g, Fats: 9 g

4.26 Warming Pumpkin Soup

Prep Time: 15 Mins, Cook Time: 15 Mins, Servings: 4

Ingredients

- 2 tbsps coconut oil
- 1 chopped brown onion, carrots chopped
- 2 cups diced pumpkin & coconut milk canned
- 1 tsp nutmeg ground & dried thyme
- Salt & pepper

Method

- In a large saucepan, melt the coconut oil over low to medium heat. Put in the pumpkin, onion, and carrot.
- Keep tossing while cooking until the veggies are tender. Add the other ingredients and reduce the heat to low after stirring. Puree the soup with a stick blender once the veggies are tender. Serve.

Nutritional Facts: Calories: 225 Kcal, Protein: 7 g, Carbs: 39 g, Fats: 7.3 g

4.27 Easy Spicy Chicken

Prep Time: 10 Mins, Cook Time: 20 Mins, Servings: 4

Ingredients

- 2 lb fillets chicken thigh
- ½ tsp pepper & salt
- 2 tbsps masala garam
- 2 tbsps powder curry
- 1 cup Greek yogurt full fat

Method

- Put everything in a big glass dish except the chicken. Put in the chicken and coat it well with the marinade.
- Refrigerate the bowl, covered, for at least an hour. Turn the oven temperature up to 400 degrees Fahrenheit. Prepare an oven tray by greasing it and lining it with aluminum foil. Put in the oven and bake for about 20 mins, till done. Include greens in your dish.

Nutritional Facts: Calories: 249 Kcal, Protein: 43 g, Carbs: 10 g, Fats: 6 g

4.28 Quick and Tasty Chicken Drumsticks

Prep Time: 10 Mins, Cook Time: 15 Mins, Servings: 5

Ingredients

- 10 drumsticks chicken
- ¼ cup oil olive
- 2 tsp paprika & salt
- 1 minced garlic clove finely
- ¼ tsp cinnamon & pepper

Method

- Put everything in a big glass dish except the chicken. Put in the chicken and coat it well with the marinade.
- Refrigerate the bowl, covered, for at least an hour. Turn the oven temperature up to 400 degrees Fahrenheit. Prepare an oven tray by greasing it and lining it with aluminum foil. Put in the oven and bake for about 20 mins, till done. Include greens in your dish.

Nutritional Facts: Calories: 480 Kcal, Protein: 72 g, Carbs: 18 g, Fats: 15 g

4.29 Simple Garlic Lemon Chicken

Prep Time: 10 Mins, Cook Time: 20 Mins, Servings: 2

Ingredients

- 2 sliced chicken breasts
- 2 minced cloves garlic
- 2 tbsp lemon juice & grated
- 1 tbsp ghee & olive oil
- ½ tsp oregano dried

Method

- Melt the fat (oil or ghee) in a large pan over moderate heat. Put in the lemon zest, lemon juice, and chopped garlic.
- Add the chicken to the pan and season with oregano. Put the cover on the pan and let it simmer for about five mins.
- Cook the chicken on both sides until it reaches an internal temperature of 165 degrees. Accompany with steamed and roasted veggies or a salad.

Nutritional Facts: Calories: 201 Kcal, Protein: 22 g, Carbs: 18 g, Fats: 4 g

4.30 Pumpkin and walnut salad

Prep Time: 10 Mins, Cook Time: 15 Mins, Servings: 4

Ingredients

- 2 cups peeled pumpkin cubed
- 2 large spinach leaves
- 1/3 cup walnut halves toasted
- 1 cup halved cherry tomatoes
- 2 tbsps lime juice & olive oil

Method

- Get the oven ready by heating it to 370 degrees Fahrenheit.
- Cut the pumpkin into cubes and spread them out on an oiled or lined baking sheet. Season with pepper and salt, then brush with olive oil.
- Roast until a golden color is achieved. Spinach, tomatoes, walnuts, and pumpkin should all be tossed together in a serving dish.
- Before serving, top with oil and a squeeze of lime.

Nutritional Facts: Calories: 506 Kcal, Protein: 11 g, Carbs: 32 g, Fats: 36 g

4.31 Chicken and Apple Salad

Prep Time: 05 Mins, Cook Time: 10 Mins, Servings: 2

Ingredients

- 2 cups cubed cooked chicken
- 1 red apple, sliced stalks of celery & Lebanese cucumber
- 1/3 cup pecans toasted
- 6 shredded lettuce leaves
- 2 tbsps olive oil & lime juice fresh

Method

- Throw everything into a serving dish, excluding the lime juice & olive oil. Pour oil & juice over the mixture, stir, then serve.

Nutritional Facts: Calories: 230 Kcal, Protein: 20 g, Carbs: 30 g, Fats: 2.5 g

4.32 Tuna and Tahini Salad

Prep Time: 10 Mins, Cook Time: 15 Mins, Servings: 2

Ingredients

- 2 cans of drained tuna
- 2 large arugula leaves, large grated carrot
- 1 cup tahini, halved cherry tomatoes & poppy seeds
- 1 sliced Lebanese cucumber
- ¼ cup lemon juice, Salt & pepper

Method

- Toss together everything in the bowl except the lemon juice & tahini.
- Put the tahini & lemon juice in a medium bowl & mix them well with a whisk.
- Douse a salad with it and serve.

Nutritional Facts: Calories: 182 Kcal, Protein: 25 g, Carbs: 6 g, Fats: 6 g

4.33 Tuna and Walnut Salad

Prep Time: 15 Mins, Cook Time: 10 Mins, Servings: 2

Ingredients

- 1 can large tuna
- 2 tbsp finely chopped fresh dill
- 1 cup halved raw walnut & cherry tomatoes
- 2 sliced stalks celery, lettuce leaves & avocado
- ¼ cup olive oil & lemon juice

Method

- Flake the tuna with a fork after draining it and placing it in a bowl.
- Mix in everything else (except the olive oil & lemon juice) and mix gently.
- Serve with a splash of lemon juice & oil on top.

Nutritional Facts: Calories: 419 Kcal, Protein: 29 g, Carbs: 13 g, Fats: 31 g

4.34 Chili Chicken Soup

Prep Time: 10 Mins, Cook Time: 10 Mins, Servings: 4

Ingredients

- 3 cups leftover cooked chicken, chopped
- 1 diced red onion, crushed cloves garlic
- 2 tbsps each of olive oil, cayenne pepper, ground cumin, Salt & pepper
- 2 sliced stalks celery, large carrots, seeds removed & sliced jalapeno pepper
- 2 cups peeled pumpkin, chopped

Method

- The garlic and onions should be cooked in olive oil till soft in a large stockpot. Replace the chicken and broth with the remaining ingredients.
- Stir constantly for 2 mins. Once the veggies have reached the desired tenderness, add the other ingredients and reduce the heat to a low setting.

Nutritional Facts: Calories: 143 Kcal, Protein: 14 g, Carbs: 18 g, Fats: 1.8 g

4.35 Chicken and Grape Salad

Prep Time: 10 Mins, Cook Time: 20 Mins, Servings: 4

Ingredients

- 1 lb cooked chicken leftover
- 2 sliced ripe tomatoes & hard-boiled eggs
- 2 sliced avocado & stalks of celery
- ½ cup pecans chopped toasted
- 2 tbsps olive oil & lemon juice

Method

- Put everything for the salad into a dish and stir it together gently.
- Gently combine with the oil & lemon juice, then serve.

Nutritional Facts: Calories: 535 Kcal, Protein: 43 g, Carbs: 8 g, Fats: 38 g

4.36 Vegetarian Quinoa Pilaf

Prep Time: 10 Mins, Cook Time: 10 Mins, Servings: 4

Ingredients

- 4 cups of olive oil, quinoa & vegetable stock
- 1 medium chopped red pepper, broccoli head & yellow pepper
- 6 thinly sliced carrots, halved cherry tomatoes & chopped medium zucchini
- 1 cup diced pumpkin, chopped onion
- 1 tbsp ground cumin, dried oregano, Salt, pepper & tomato paste

Method

- Cook the quinoa in a large saucepan with the veggie stock for about fifteen minutes until it has softened after rinsing it.
- Olive oil should be heated in a large saucepan over medium heat. Fry the onion for about three mins or until it softens.
- Replace the quinoa with the remaining ingredients.
- Cook the veggies slowly, stirring occasionally, until they are tender. If the veggies are scorching on the bottom of the pan, you might need to add extra water.
- When the vegetables are done cooking, add them to the quinoa.
- Blend and serve.

Nutritional Facts: Calories: 120 Kcal, Protein: 5 g, Carbs: 19 g, Fats: 3 g

4.37 Chicken and Orange Salad

Prep Time: 10 Mins, Cook Time: 15 Mins, Servings: 4

Ingredients

- 2 oranges, peeled and sliced
- 1 cooked chicken
- 4 lettuce handfuls
- 2 sliced Lebanese cucumber, sliced stalks celery & chopped ripe tomatoes
- ¼ cup olive oil & fresh lemon juice

Method

- In a large bowl, combine all of the salad ingredients.
- Dress with olive oil & lemon juice, then toss
- Serve

Nutritional Facts: Calories: 410 Kcal, Protein: 38 g, Carbs: 41 g, Fats: 13 g

4.38 Succulent Lamb Skewers

Prep Time: 05 Mins, Cook Time: 25 Mins, Servings: 4

Ingredients

- 1 & ½ lbs of ground lamb
- 2 minced brown onion & cloves garlic
- 1 handful finely chopped mint fresh leaves & parsley leaves
- 2 tsps ground cumin & coriander
- Salt & pepper

Method

- Skewers may be made of metal or bamboo; if using bamboo, soak it in water the night before usage.
- Start by preheating the oven to 375 degrees F. Put everything in a big bowl and mix it up with your hands until fully combined. Form sausage-like skewers out of the meat.
- Put the skewers in a single layer on a baking sheet, then bake for 30 mins, till done. The skewers' cooking duration will be proportional to their size.

Nutritional Facts: Calories: 414 Kcal, Protein: 33 g, Carbs: 45 g, Fats: 10 g

4.39 Tuna and Avocado Salad

Prep Time: 10 Mins, Cook Time: 15 Mins, Servings: 1

Ingredients

- 1 sliced small avocado
- 5 ozs of drained canned tuna
- 2 handful large lettuce leaves, red onion, radishes
- ½ cup parmesan cheese & halved cherry tomatoes
- 1 tbsp Italian dried herbs & vinegar apple cider

Method

- Throw everything into a dish and serve.

Nutritional Facts: Calories: 314 Kcal, Protein: 35 g, Carbs: 11 g, Fats: 17 g

4.40 Simple Chicken and Quinoa Salad

Prep Time: 10 Mins, Cook Time: 15 Mins, Servings: 2

Ingredients

- 1 diced chicken breast
- 2 large spinach leaves handful & sliced avocado
- 1 cup halved cherry tomatoes & cooked quinoa
- 2 tbsps each olive oil and lemon juice

- Salt & pepper

Method

- Prepare the chicken by sautéing it in olive oil in a skillet over medium heat.
- Combine celery, avocado, spinach, tomatoes, and quinoa in a serving dish.
- Toss once more before adding the lemon juice, olive oil, cooked chicken, salt, & pepper. Serve.

Nutritional Facts: Calories: 295 Kcal, Protein: 20 g, Carbs: 19 g, Fats: 15 g

4.41 Low-Carb Salmon Salad

Prep Time: 05 Mins, Cook Time: 0 Mins, Servings: 1

Ingredients

- 6 oz can salmon, drained
- 1 sliced boiled egg
- ½ cup sliced cherry tomatoes
- 2 sliced lettuce leaves, small avocado & red radishes
- 1 tbsp mustard Dijon, sliced capers & fresh parsley

Method

- To serve, mix all the ingredients in a bowl.

Nutritional Facts: Calories: 441 Kcal, Protein: 23 g, Carbs: 5.5 g, Fats: 36 g

4.42 Roast Cauliflower and Quinoa Salad

Prep Time: 05 Mins, Cook Time: 20 Mins, Servings: 2

Ingredients

- ½ chopped head of cauliflower
- 1 tbsp oil olive
- 1 cup quinoa cooked
- 1 handful chopped parsley leaves
- ¼ cup cumin ground& pecans toasted

Method

- Put in a preheated 395-degree oven.
- Oil and cumin should be drizzled over the cauliflower on a buttered baking sheet. Toss in the oven and cook until the edges are brown.
- Gently mix all the ingredients in a bowl.

Nutritional Facts: Calories: 388 Kcal, Protein: 13 g, Carbs: 54 g, Fats: 15 g

4.43 Baked Lime and Chili Chicken

Prep Time: 05 Mins, Cook Time: 25 Mins, Servings: 4

Ingredients

- 2 lbs drumsticks chicken
- 4 tbsps oil olive
- 2 crushed cloves garlic
- 2 tbsps juice lime & lime zest grated
- 2 tsps chili flakes

Method

- Whisk together all ingredients in a glass bowl, except for the chicken drumsticks. Toss in the drumsticks, cover, and chill for at least 2 hours.
- Turn the oven temperature up to 375°F.
- Prepare a oiled baking sheet and lay out the chicken drumsticks. Cook for 25 mins, till the juices flow clear when punctured in the thickest portion of the drumsticks. Drumsticks should be flipped over halfway through the cooking time.
- Eat with a side of salad.

Nutritional Facts: Calories: 128 Kcal, Protein: 18 g, Carbs: 12 g, Fats: 0.6 g

4.44 Chicken Grapefruit Salad

Prep Time: 10 Mins, Cook Time: 10 Mins, Servings: 2

Ingredients

- 2 cups cooked chicken shredded/diced
- 1 peeled & sliced pink grapefruit
- 1 large handful of arugula & sliced avocado
- 1 cup Sliced cherry tomatoes & stalks celery
- 4 tbsps grapefruit juice & olive oil

Method

- Put everything for the salad into a serving dish. Grapefruit juice & olive oil may be used as a dressing for this dish.

Nutritional Facts: Calories: 710 Kcal, Protein: 45 g, Carbs: 31 g, Fats: 46 g

4.45 Crispy Chicken With Brussels Sprouts

Prep Time: 05 Mins, Cook Time: 25 Mins, Servings: 2

Ingredients

- 2 large legs of chicken
- 10 sprouts Brussels
- 2 tbsps fresh parsley, finely chopped
- ¼ cup juice lemon, olive oil or pastured ghee
- Herbanare or Salt

Method

- Turn the oven temperature up to 425 degrees Fahrenheit.
- The chicken legs should be washed and patted dry. Add some salt or Herbamare to give them flavor. Put the chicken legs in a hot pan with a tbsp of ghee. Brown & crisp them up on both sides in the oven.
- Put the chicken legs aside.
- The Brussels sprouts should be diced and added to the skillet after a tsp of ghee is added. They need around 3 mins in the oven.
- Combine everything in a baking dish & bake for around 30 mins, till the chicken is fully cooked.
- Eat with a side of salad.

Nutritional Facts: Calories: 235 Kcal, Protein: 30 g, Carbs: 12 g, Fats: 8 g

4.46 Grain-Free Shepherd's Pie

Prep Time: 05 Mins, Cook Time: 30 Mins, Servings: 4

Ingredients

- 2 diced clove garlic, carrots & brown onion
- 1 lb ground beef
- ½ cup chopped pumpkin
- 2 tsp tomato paste, dried rosemary & ground cumin
- 2 tbsps oil olive

Method

- Onion and garlic should be sautéed in olive oil over medium heat until softening. For another 5 mins, while stirring occasionally, add the pumpkin and carrot.
- Cook the meat with the spices and salt until it is done, stirring occasionally. Simmer for about 10 mins after adding the tomato paste & stock or water.
- Prepare a 350°F oven.
- Place filling in an oiled casserole dish and bake.

- Mix all the ingredients for the potato filling in a little bowl. Put the potato mixture on top of the meat mixture and bake.

- Put it in the oven for about 30 mins, till it browns.

Nutritional Facts: Calories: 560 Kcal, Protein: 27 g, Carbs: 82 g, Fats: 13 g

Chapter 5: Nourishing Dinners for Your Liver

Here are some nourishing dinner recipes to purify your liver to regain health and energy.

5.1 Lamb Cutlets with Peach Salad

Prep Time: 05 Mins, Cook Time: 20 Mins, Servings: 4

Ingredients

- 12 lamb cutlets
- 2 sliced peaches
- 4 handfuls roughly chopped arugula leaves
- 1 tbsp crushed cumin seeds & balsamic vinegar
- ½ cup of pecans, olive oil & goat fetta cubed cheese

Method

- Add the cumin & olive oil to the lamb cutlets and mix well. Salt & pepper to taste.
- Lamb cutlets may be cooked perfectly in a skillet or on the grill.
- To prepare, heat a frying pan or grill to medium heat and cook your peach wedges for about 2 mins each side.
- Distribute the peaches between plates. Lamb cutlets should be placed on plates, then the peaches & the rest of the salad should be added.

Nutritional Facts: Calories: 361 Kcal, Protein: 32 g, Carbs: 22 g, Fats: 16 g

5.2 Dairy-Free Lemon and Mustard Turkey Thighs

Prep Time: 10 Mins, Cook Time: 20 Mins, Servings: 4

Ingredients

- 4 thighs turkey
- ½ cup juice of lemon
- ¼ cup dried oregano & tahini
- 2 tbsps mustard Dijon
- Salt & pepper

Method

- In a pan over a medium-high flame, warm the oil. Add pepper and salt to the turkey before cooking.
- Put the turkey in a pan and let it sizzle for a while.
- Put the rest of the ingredients in a bowl and mix them. Flip the turkey over, add the sauce, and cook on low with the top off.
- Turkey has to be cooked for about 20 mins to ensure it is well done.

Nutritional Facts: Calories: 667 Kcal, Protein: 49 g, Carbs: 18 g, Fats: 42 g

5.3 Zucchini and Salmon Slice

Prep Time: 05 Mins, Cook Time: 20 Mins, Servings: 3

Ingredients

- 6 whisked eggs
- ¼ cup flour coconut
- 2 finely diced brown onion, a coarsely grated slice of pumpkin & large zucchinis
- ½ cup of olive oil, sliced, finely diced brown onion & smoked salmon
- 2 tsps parsley, dried

Method

- Turn the oven temperature up to 355.
- Prepare a oiled baking dish.
- Combine everything and put it on a plate.
- Set & slightly brown in the oven, which should take around 20 mins.
- Eat with a side of salad.

Nutritional Facts: Calories: 278 Kcal, Protein: 23 g, Carbs: 18 g, Fats: 13 g

5.4 Baked Salmon with Avocado Salad

Prep Time: 10 Mins, Cook Time: 15 Mins, Servings: 1

Ingredients

- 1 portion fresh salmon
- 2 tbsps ghee or olive oil
- 1 clove minced garlic
- 2 tbsps lime juice or lemon

Method

- Mix the minced garlic, citrus juice, and oil/animal fat in a large bowl.
- Incorporate the salmon and coat it well with the marinade. Cover the bowl in the refrigerator for at least two hours.
- Grill the salmon over moderate heat until it reaches the doneness you choose.
- Dress the salad with lemon juice & olive oil, then place the salmon on top.

Nutritional Facts: Calories: 271 Kcal, Protein: 23 g, Carbs: 4 g, Fats: 17 g

5.5 Low-Carb Garlic & Rosemary Chicken Thighs

Prep Time: 10 Mins, Cook Time: 20 Mins, Servings: 4

Ingredients

- 4 fillets of chicken thigh
- 2 minced cloves garlic
- 2 tsps rosemary, dried
- 2 tbsps lemon Juice & oil olive
- 1 tsp of salt

Method

- The chicken thighs should be dried using paper towels.
- Put the thighs in a bowl and drizzle the lemon juice over them. Set aside fifteen to twenty mins for cooling the chicken.
- Mix everything except the olive oil and coat the chicken.
- Put your olive oil in a large skillet and heat it over medium.
- Ensure the chicken thighs are fully done by cooking them on both sides.
- Eat with a side of salad.

Nutritional Facts: Calories: 469 Kcal, Protein: 45 g, Carbs: 7 g, Fats: 28 g

5.6 Chicken and Pepper Stir Fry

Prep Time: 15 Mins, Cook Time: 15 Mins, Servings: 4

Ingredients

- 1 lb chicken, ground
- 2 tbsps ghee or olive oil & soy sauce or tamari
- 4 tbsps lemon juice, fresh
- 1 handful cashews, roasted & fresh torn basil leaves
- 1 tbsp coconut aminos or sliced red pepper

Method

- Warm the ghee or olive oil in a deep-frying pan.
- Stir-fry the chicken for a few mins or until it reaches an internal temperature of 165 degrees Fahrenheit.
- Toss in some pepper.
- Keep cooking for a few more mins, then throw in everything except the basil.
- Remove the mixture from the heat and add the basil leaves.
- Serve.

Nutritional Facts: Calories: 480 Kcal, Protein: 26 g, Carbs: 51 g, Fats: 19 g

5.7 Spicy Ginger Chicken

Prep Time: 10 Mins, Cook Time: 20 Mins, Servings: 4

Ingredients

- 1 & ½ lbs chicken drumsticks
- 1 small diced brown onion
- ½ sliced red pepper capsicum & fresh ginger
- ½ tsp of cayenne pepper & salt
- 1 tbsp ghee & olive oil

Method

- Over medium heat, melt the oil and ghee in a pan. The onion & ginger should be cooked for around 3 mins. Substitute the chicken with the other ingredients and close the lid.
- Toss in the chicken, reduce the heat to a low simmer and whisk everything together. For about 25 mins, stirring periodically, till the chicken is fully cooked. Add a little water if the mixture seems to be drying out too much.
- Eat with a side of salad.

Nutritional Facts: Calories: 349 Kcal, Protein: 22 g, Carbs: 40 g, Fats: 11 g

5.8 Low-Carb Salmon with Green Beans

Prep Time: 10 Mins, Cook Time: 10 Mins, Servings: 2

Ingredients

- 2 large green beans handfuls fresh
- 2 portions of salmon fresh
- 2 tbsps ghee or butter
- half a Juice of lemon

Method

- Green beans should be steamed until their color brightens somewhat.
- In a skillet, melt the butter over a medium-high flame. Cook your salmon fillets for about 4 mins on each side in a pan.
- Add the lemon juice and green beans just before serving with the fish. Cook for a further min while stirring.
- Add salt, and you're ready to serve.

Nutritional Facts: Calories: 480 Kcal, Protein: 31 g, Carbs: 38 g, Fats: 23 g

5.9 Low-Carb Lemon Turkey Breasts

Prep Time: 10 Mins, Cook Time: 20 Mins, Servings: 4

Ingredients

- 4 breasts turkey
- ½ cup juice lemon
- ¼ cup of tahini
- 2 tbsps mustard Dijon
- ghee or olive oil, Extra virgin

Method

- Warm a frying pan with oil or lard over a medium-high flame. Add pepper and salt to the turkey before cooking.
- Put the turkey in a pan and let it sizzle for a while.
- Put the rest of the ingredients in a bowl and mix them. Flip the turkey over, add the sauce, and cook on low with the top off.
- Turkey has to be cooked for about 20 mins to ensure it is well done.

Nutritional Facts: Calories: 162 Kcal, Protein: 35 g, Carbs: 2 g, Fats: 1 g

5.10 Pumpkin and Zucchini Frittata

Prep Time: 10 Mins, Cook Time: 25 Mins, Servings: 2

Ingredients

- 6 whisked eggs
- ¼ cup finely diced brown onion & almond meal
- 2 coarsely grated slices of pumpkin & large zucchinis
- ¼ cup finely chopped red pepper (capsicum)
- ¼ cup dried parsley & sliced pitted olives & olive oil

Method

- Turn the oven temperature up to 355.
- Prepare a oiled baking dish.
- Combine everything and put it on a plate.
- Set slightly brown in the oven, which should take around 30 mins.
- Eat with a side of salad.

Nutritional Facts: Calories: 71 Kcal, Protein: 6 g, Carbs: 4 g, Fats: 3 g

5.11 Oregano Pork Chops

Prep Time: 10 Mins, Cook Time: 20 Mins, Servings: 3

Ingredients

- 6 chops pork
- 2 tbsps olive oil or ghee, lard
- 1 tbsp oregano, dried
- Salt & pepper

Method

- Over medium heat, put the lard, ghee, or olive oil in a skillet.
- Put pepper and salt on the pork chops.
- After heating the pan, add the pork chops and some oregano. Chops should be cooked well & browned on all sides.
- Serve.

Nutritional Facts: Calories: 510 Kcal, Protein: 49 g, Carbs: 33 g, Fats: 19 g

5.12 Baked Paprika Chicken

Prep Time: 10 Mins, Cook Time: 30 Mins, Servings: 4

Ingredients

- 2 lbs pieces of chicken
- 2 lbs peeled & chopped pumpkin & sprig rosemary
- 1 tbsp powdered paprika
- ¼ cup nuts, pine
- 4 tbsps of olive oil

Method

- Turn the oven temperature to 400°F.
- Coat an oven-safe dish with the butter and add the chicken & pumpkin.
- Use a pastry brush to apply the olive oil on them.
- Salt, pepper, and paprika should be distributed equally over the chicken & pumpkin.
- Place a sprig of rosemary in it.
- Put the dish in an oven-safe foil and bake.
- The baking time is 30 mins.
- Take the foil off, toss in some pine nuts, and roast the chicken until it's done.

Nutritional Facts: Calories: 465 Kcal, Protein: 30 g, Carbs: 35 g, Fats: 22 g

5.13 Lime Tuna Steaks

Prep Time: 10 Mins, Cook Time: 10 Mins, Servings: 2

Ingredients

- 5 oz steaks of tuna
- 1 tbsp each coconut oil & butter or ghee
- 1 lime Zest & juice
- Salt & pepper

Method

- Oil and ghee should be heated in a pan on medium heat. Toss in the lime zest and give the mixture a good toss. Salt and pepper the tuna steaks before adding them to the pan.
- Squeeze the lime and add the juice to the pot.
- The recommended cooking time for tuna steaks is 2 mins each side.
- Toss the tuna with the leftover lime juice off the pan, then serve alongside a salad and vegetables.

Nutritional Facts: Calories: 363 Kcal, Protein: 51 g, Carbs: 3 g, Fats: 16 g

5.14 Dairy Free Creamy Salmon

Prep Time: 05 Mins, Cook Time: 10 Mins, Servings: 2

Ingredients

- 2 fresh salmon pieces
- 1 tbsp tamari or coconut aminos
- ¼ cup of full-fat coconut milk, canned
- 1 tbsp lime juice, freshly squeezed
- ½ tsp lime zest, fresh

Method

- Put everything in a pan except the salmon and cook it over medium. When the sauce is almost at a boil, add the fish.
- Salmon typically takes around 2 mins on each side to cook to perfection.
- Accompany with greens or steamed veggies.

Nutritional Facts: Calories: 540 Kcal, Protein: 39 g, Carbs: 7 g, Fats: 34 g

5.15 Chicken with Olives

Prep Time: 10 Mins, Cook Time: 20 Mins, Servings: 2

Ingredients

- 2 chicken breasts
- 2 sliced red capsicum, brown onion, cloves garlic (each)
- 4 medium quartered button squash
- 1 can tomatoes, diced
- 2 Tbsp each black olives, olive oil, sweet paprika, dried oregano & capers

Method

- Set oven temperature to 390 degrees Fahrenheit.
- Fry some chicken breasts in a skillet with olive oil and hot coals. When browned, take off the heat.
- Throw the rest of the stuff into a bowl and mix it up. Place chicken breasts on top and transfer to a baking tray.
- Wrap in foil and cook for 20 mins at 400 degrees. After 10 mins, take the foil off and continue cooking.
- Eat with a side of salad.

Nutritional Facts: Calories: 386 Kcal, Protein: 45 g, Carbs: 3 g, Fats: 21 g

5.16 Low-Carb Garlic Chicken

Prep Time: 05 Mins, Cook Time: 20 Mins, Servings: 4

Ingredients

- 1 lb pieces chicken
- 2 tbsps each dried oregano, olive oil
- 4 garlic cloves, minced
- 2 cups each spinach leaves, chopped broccoli florets
- ¼ cup cream coconut

Method

- Olive oil should be heated in a big pan over a medium-high flame. The chicken should be diced and seasoned with oregano, garlic, salt, and pepper.
- Stir the chicken till it is completely done.
- Cook your broccoli until it reaches the doneness you choose, then add the additional ingredients.
- Serve

Nutritional Facts: Calories: 496 Kcal, Protein: 45 g, Carbs: 7 g, Fats: 28 g

5.17 Pork and Apple Skewers

Prep Time: 10 Mins, Cook Time: 05 Mins, Servings: 6

Ingredients

- 1 & ½ lb pork
- 1 sliced green apple, capsicum red pepper
- ¼ cup each of balsamic vinegar, olive oil, lime juice & freshly squeezed
- Salt & pepper
- 6 skewers

Method

- Combine the vinegar, salt, olive oil, lime juice, and pepper in a glass bowl.
- Put the pork cubes in the marinade and sit in the refrigerator for two hours.
- Turn on the grill or barbecue to medium heat.
- Meat, apple, & pepper should all be skewered together. Cook for about 5 mins on every side of a grill or barbecue until done.

Nutritional Facts: Calories: 320 Kcal, Protein: 19 g, Carbs: 14 g, Fats: 22 g

5.18 Low-Carb Ribeye with Garlic Sauce

Prep Time: 10 Mins, Cook Time: 10 Mins, Servings: 2

Ingredients

- 2 steaks ribeye
- Salt & pepper

Method

- The steaks should be seasoned and then pan-fried to the desired doneness.
- Sauce ingredients may be mixed in a food processor or blender while the steaks rest. Mix until everything is uniform.
- Serve the steaks with the sauce drizzled on top.

Nutritional Facts: Calories: 310 Kcal, Protein: 18 g, Carbs: 3 g, Fats: 25 g

5.19 Mediterranean Style Chicken

Prep Time: 10 Mins, Cook Time: 20 Mins, Servings: 4

Ingredients

- 8 pieces chicken thigh
- 2 tsp each paprika & dried oregano
- 3 tbsps chopped sundried tomatoes
- ¼ cup each olive oil & lemon juice

- Salt & pepper

Method

- Start by preheating the oven to 375°F. Put everything in a dish except the chicken. Spread the chicken out on a baking sheet that has been buttered.

- Marinate the chicken by covering each piece well with the marinade.

- To bake the chicken, put it in the oven & bake it for around twenty to thirty mins. The chicken parts' size will dictate how long they need to bake.

Nutritional Facts: Calories: 338 Kcal, Protein: 31 g, Carbs: 8 g, Fats: 20 g

5.20 Spicy Beef Skewers

Prep Time: 10 Mins, Cook Time: 10 Mins, Servings: 4

Ingredients

- 1 lb beef, diced

- 2 tbsps each olive oil, lime juice

- ¼ cup coconut aminos or tamari

- 1 each crushed clove garlic & small red chili

- 1 sliced red onion, large

Method

- Everything save the steak and onion should be put into a big glass bowl. The meat should be added and mixed with your hands so the marinade may penetrate all the pieces. Cover the bowl.

- The grill should be preheated to medium heat. After marinating, drain the steak and tie it over skewers, alternately with onion cubes.

- Allow the skewers to roast on the grill for around 10 mins.

Nutritional Facts: Calories: 210 Kcal, Protein: 26 g, Carbs: 11 g, Fats: 6 g

5.21 Grilled Garlic Chicken

Prep Time: 15 Mins, Cook Time: 10 Mins, Servings: 4

Ingredients

- 2 lbs thighs, chicken

- ½ cup olive oil & balsamic vinegar

- 4 minced garlic cloves

- ½ tsp oregano, dried

- Salt & pepper

Method

- Combine everything in a glass dish except the chicken. Insert chicken thighs and ensure that the marinade completely covers them. Put the bowl in the freezer overnight with the lid on.
- Turn on the grill's heat to medium. Cook your chicken for about 10 mins on each side on a hot grill or until they are fully done.
- Eat with a side of salad.

Nutritional Facts: Calories: 468 Kcal, Protein: 59 g, Carbs: 10 g, Fats: 18 g

5.22 Keto Lemon Chicken Wings

Prep Time: 15 Mins, Cook Time: 15 Mins, Servings: 4

Ingredients

- 2 lbs wings, chicken
- 1 tsp of salt
- 1 tbsp of lemon zest & juice lemon
- ¼ cup melted ghee or olive oil

Method

- Set oven temperature to 375°F.
- Chicken wings, please. Spread the wings evenly on a prepared baking sheet, ensuring they won't touch each other.
- Put the wings into the oven and bake them for about 15 mins on each side. The quantity of wings you utilize and the size of your oven will determine how long they need to be cooked.
- In a bowl, mix up the other ingredients while the wings cook.
- When the wings are cooked, toss into the oil & lemon mixture until fully coated.

Nutritional Facts: Calories: 222 Kcal, Protein: 20 g, Carbs: 2 g, Fats: 15 g

5.23 Lemon and Mint Lamb Chops

Prep Time: 10 Mins, Cook Time: 20 Mins, Servings: 2

Ingredients

- 4 lamb chops T-bone loin
- 2 tbsps fresh mint, finely chopped
- 1 clove garlic, crushed
- 1 tbsp each dried thyme & olive oil
- ¼ cup juice of lemon

Method

- Salt and pepper on both sides of the lamb chops.
- Combine the remaining ingredients in a small blender or grinder for a smooth mixture.
- Put your lamb chops in a glass dish and coat them with the marinade. Put in the refrigerator overnight covered.
- The following day, grill them over a medium-high flame until they reach the desired doneness.
- Eat with a side of salad.

Nutritional Facts: Calories: 436 Kcal, Protein: 48 g, Carbs: 2 g, Fats: 25 g

5.24 One Pan Chicken Dinner

Prep Time: 05 Mins, Cook Time: 10 Mins, Servings: 4

Ingredients

- 1 lb thighs chicken
- 1 each sliced brown onion, sliced carrots, head cauliflower
- ½ cup each lemon zest, lemon juice & pitted Kalamata olives
- 3 tbsps dried oregano & ghee or olive oil
- ½ tsp of salt

Method

- Bake at 400 degrees Fahrenheit, preheated.
- Spread the chicken out on a baking sheet. Put everything over the chicken except the lemon juice & olive oil.
- Spread oil & juice over the chicken, then bake for about 50 mins, till the chicken is fully done.

Nutritional Facts: Calories: 388 Kcal, Protein: 21 g, Carbs: 15 g, Fats: 28 g

5.25 Tasty chicken skewers

Prep Time: 10 Mins, Cook Time: 15 Mins, Servings: 4

Ingredients

- 4 breasts chicken
- 1 tsp oregano dried
- Salt & pepper
- for cooking Olive oil

Method

- Prepare a medium fire in the grill. Put the chicken pieces on the skewers.
- Chicken pieces seasoned with lemon juice, oregano, salt, and pepper.

- Grill the chicken for about 5 mins on every side, till it's cooked through, after spraying both sides with olive oil. Eat with a side of salad.

Nutritional Facts: Calories: 220 Kcal, Protein: 15 g, Carbs: 35 g, Fats: 2 g

5.26 Salmon and Tomato Salad

Prep Time: 15 Mins, Cook Time: 15 Mins, Servings: 4

Ingredients

- 1 large salmon fillet, fresh
- 1 clove minced garlic
- 1 cup halved cherry tomatoes
- 2 large, roughly chopped handfuls of arugula
- 2 tbsps each melted ghee, lemon juice & olive oil

Method

- Grill to medium-high temperature. Add pepper and salt to both sides of the fish after brushing it with ghee.
- Mince some garlic and sprinkle it on top of the fish. Prepare the fish for the grill by wrapping it in foil.
- Salmon is ready when it easily flakes. This usually takes around 15 mins. Throw the rest into a serving dish and mix it around lightly.
- Break the salmon into little pieces after it has cooled enough to handle & sprinkle it over the salad.

Nutritional Facts: Calories: 488 Kcal, Protein: 39 g, Carbs: 7 g, Fats: 34 g

5.27 Salmon and Beet Salad

Prep Time: 15 Mins, Cook Time: 15 Mins, Servings: 2

Ingredients

- 6 oz drained salmon, canned
- 2 each medium cooked diced beet, sliced red radishes, diced avocado & large lettuce leaves handfuls torn
- 1 snow pea handful
- ½ sliced red onion small
- ¼ cup parsley finely chopped

Method

- The salmon should be flaked and placed in a serving dish. Add the remaining salad ingredients & mix lightly to combine. To serve, drizzle salad with dressing.

Nutritional Facts: Calories: 525 Kcal, Protein: 48 g, Carbs: 28 g, Fats: 26 g

5.28 Egg and Avocado Salad

Prep Time: 15 Mins, Cook Time: 15 Mins, Servings: 2

Ingredients

- 4 sliced boiled eggs
- 2 sliced avocado, red radishes & smoked salmon
- 2 large, shredded handfuls lettuce
- 1 diced large carrot
- 2 tbsps each of lemon juice & olive oil

Method

- Toss the salad ingredients together in a bowl. To serve, drizzle with dressing.

Nutritional Facts: Calories: 170 Kcal, Protein: 8 g, Carbs: 7 g, Fats: 12 g

5.29 Healthy Chicken Schnitzel

Prep Time: 15 Mins, Cook Time: 15 Mins, Servings: 4

Ingredients

- 2 sliced chicken breasts
- 2 lightly whisked eggs
- ½ cup each arrowroot or tapioca flour & coconut flour
- 1 cup ground cumin & almond meal
- ½ tsp of salt

Method

- Use a meat tenderizer to flatten the chicken breasts. To a small bowl, add the whisked eggs.
- Put tapioca flour in one bowl, the coconut flour in another, the almond flour in another, and the cumin and salt in another.
- Coat each piece of chicken in tapioca flour, then in the beaten eggs, and last in the almond meal.
- Put the chicken in an ovenproof dish, coat side up, and chill for 15 minutes.
- To ensure the chicken is cooked, sauté it in a skillet with ghee, olive oil, and coconut oil on both sides. Eat with a side of salad.

Nutritional Facts: Calories: 667 Kcal, Protein: 48 g, Carbs: 67 g, Fats: 23 g

5.30 Roast Pumpkin And Chicken Salad

Prep Time: 05 Mins, Cook Time: 25 Mins, Servings: 3

Ingredients

- 2 diced chicken breasts cooked
- 1 cup each of raw pumpkin diced & halved cherry tomatoes
- 2 sliced cloves garlic, red onion, capsicum red pepper
- 1 handful rocket arugula
- Olive oil

Method

- Put in a preheated 390-degree oven.
- Prepare a baking sheet by arranging the pumpkin and garlic in dice. Toss with olive oil & roast at 400° for about 30 mins, till tender and golden.
- Mix everything in a big salad dish. Pour some olive oil over the top and serve.

Nutritional Facts: Calories: 434 Kcal, Protein: 32 g, Carbs: 23 g, Fats: 23 g

5.31 Grilled Garlicky Chicken Drumsticks

Prep Time: 15 Mins, Cook Time: 15 Mins, Servings: 5

Ingredients

- 10 drumsticks chicken
- ¾ cup of oil olive
- 8 cloves crushed garlic
- 1 tsp lemon juice & lemon zest
- 1 tsp of salt

Method

- Put everything in a blender and food processor except the drumsticks, and whirl it around until it's completely smooth.
- Lightly slash the drumsticks with a knife to open up the meat and increase marinade absorption.
- Drumsticks and marinade should be combined in a glass dish. Rubbing the mixture with your fingertips ensures that the drumsticks have been adequately coated.
- Refrigerate the bowl, covered, for about 4 hours. Drumsticks should be grilled until fully done.

Nutritional Facts: Calories: 380 Kcal, Protein: 33 g, Carbs: 1 g, Fats: 27 g

5.32 Citrus and Coconut Salmon

Prep Time: 10 Mins, Cook Time: 10 Mins, Servings: 2

Ingredients

- 2 pieces fresh salmon
- 1 tbsp aminos coconut
- ¼ cup of coconut milk canned full-fat
- 1 tbsp orange juice, freshly squeezed
- ½ tsp fresh Sea salt, orange zest

Method

- Put everything in a pan except the salmon & cook it over medium. When the sauce is almost at a boil, add the fish.
- Salmon typically takes around 2 mins on each side to cook to perfection. Accompany with greens or steamed veggies.

Nutritional Facts: Calories: 251 Kcal, Protein: 16 g, Carbs: 26 g, Fats: 10 g

5.33 Stuffed Peppers

Prep Time: 10 Mins, Cook Time: 10 Mins, Servings: 4

Ingredients

- 4 core & seeds removed bell peppers
- 8 beaten eggs
- 1 cup of halved cherry tomatoes & diced fresh mushrooms
- 1 each coarsely grated large carrot, diced red onion,
- 1 tbsp dried oregano & olive oil

Method

- Turn the oven temperature up to 375 degrees Fahrenheit. The onion should be cooked in olive oil until it is tender.
- Continue cooking by adding the tomatoes, mushrooms, and carrots to the pan. Don't forget the seasonings!
- Stuff the peppers with the mixture, then divide the beaten egg mixture among the four peppers.
- Arrange the peppers in a single layer on a prepared baking sheet, and bake for around 40 mins.

Nutritional Facts: Calories: 140 Kcal, Protein: 7 g, Carbs: 23 g, Fats: 3 g

5.34 Slow Cooked Lamb Shanks

Prep Time: 05 Mins, Cook Time: 30 Mins, Servings: 2

Ingredients

- 2 shanks lamb
- 1 cup vegetable stock or beef
- 1 chopped brown onion
- 1 tbsp olive oil or pastured ghee
- 4 cloves garlic & sprigs finely diced fresh rosemary

Method

- Add salt and pepper to the meat and set it aside. Over a medium-high flame, sauté the shanks in the oil or ghee till lightly browned on both sides.
- Throw the hocks into a slow cooker and crock pot. In a pan, soften the garlic, onion, & rosemary in some olive oil.
- Put everything else into a crock pot and simmer for 30 mins on high.
- Accompany with a side salad or veggies.

Nutritional Facts: Calories: 370 Kcal, Protein: 39 g, Carbs: 7 g, Fats: 22 g

5.35 Rice and Vegetable Stuffed Capsicums

Prep Time: 05 Mins, Cook Time: 25 Mins, Servings: 3

Ingredients

- 6 red or green bell peppers (capsicums)
- 3 cups rice, cooked
- 2 finely chopped zucchini, large button mushrooms, small onion & roughly grated carrots
- 2 tbsps olive oil, parsley & chives, finely chopped
- ½ cup almonds flaked slivered

Method

- Get the oven up to temperature, preferably around 180C (350F).
- Remove the caps from the peppers.
- Warm some olive oil in a deep skillet. The onion must be cooked slowly until it softens. Toss in the carrot & celery, mix, and continue cooking for two more mins.
- Cook for 2 mins after adding the additional ingredients and stirring constantly.
- Stuff the peppers with cooked meat, rice, or vegetables. Put the stuffed peppers in a oiled casserole dish & replace the caps.
- Put the dish in the oven with foil covering it and bake for about 30 mins.

Nutritional Facts: Calories: 222 Kcal, Protein: 6 g, Carbs: 18 g, Fats: 14 g

5.36 Shrimp and Broccoli Stir Fry

Prep Time: 05 Mins, Cook Time: 15 Mins, Servings: 2

Ingredients

- 1 head small florets & lightly steamed broccoli
- 1 roasted cashews, large handful
- 2 tbsps each of lime juice, sesame seeds, fish sauce, coconut aminos, macadamia nut oil, olive oil or duck fat
- 2 sliced capsicum red pepper & crushed cloves garlic
- 8 oz shrimp peeled

Method

- Prepare the oil and duck fat by heating it in a skillet or wok. Mix in the cashews, garlic, sesame seeds, & red pepper. After a few mins of stir-frying, the prawns should be about done.
- Add some broccoli.
- Add 30 seconds of cooking time, then serve.

Nutritional Facts: Calories: 86 Kcal, Protein: 7 g, Carbs: 8 g, Fats: 3 g

5.37 Garlic and Thyme Chicken Thighs

Prep Time: 05 Mins, Cook Time: 25 Mins, Servings: 4

Ingredients

- 1 & ½ lbs thighs chicken
- 1 small diced brown onion
- ½ sliced capsicum red pepper
- 4 crushed cloves garlic
- 1 tsp salt & dried thyme
- 1 tbsp oil olive

Method

- Over a medium-high flame, melt the ghee, oil, and tallow into a pan. The garlic and onion should be cooked for around three mins. Substitute the chicken with the other ingredients and close the lid.
- Toss in the chicken, reduce the heat to a low simmer and whisk everything together. If the ingredients are too dry, you may add water. For about 30 mins, stirring periodically, till the chicken is fully cooked.
- Eat with a side of salad.

Nutritional Facts: Calories: 178 Kcal, Protein: 34 g, Carbs: 5 g, Fats: 4 g

5.38 Mediterranean Beef Skewers

Prep Time: 10 Mins, Cook Time: 15 Mins, Servings: 4

Ingredients

- 2 lbs diced beef
- 1 diced red pepper
- 2 crushed cloves garlic and skewers
- 1 tbsp dried thyme, oregano, marjoram
- 4 tbsps olive oil
- 2 tbsps fresh lemon

Method

- Mix everything except the meat & red pepper.
- Toss in the steak and stir until it is well coated in the marinade.
- Put the bowl in the freezer overnight with the lid on.
- Prepare a medium fire in the grill.
- Put the steak and peppers on skewers and grill for about 8 mins, till the meat is cooked to your preference.

Nutritional Facts: Calories: 267 Kcal, Protein: 15 g, Carbs: 25 g, Fats: 12 g

Chapter 6: Sweets and Treats Without the Guilt

Here are sweet and treat recipes to purify your liver to regain health and energy.

6.1 Sugar-Free Hazelnut Fudge

Prep Time: 05 Mins, Cook Time: 25 Mins, Servings: 3

Ingredients

- 1 cup butter hazelnut
- 1/3 cup coconut oil, melted
- ½ tsp extract, vanilla
- ½ tsp natural sugar or alternative Nature Sweet
- ¼ cup hazelnut pieces, roasted

Method

- Process or blend the first 4 ingredients till completely smooth.
- Combine chopped hazelnuts with the batter and spread them on a baking sheet before placing them in the freezer.
- Cut into squares before serving.

Nutritional Facts: Calories: 103 Kcal, Protein: 2 g, Carbs: 7 g, Fats: 8 g

6.2 Grain Free Carrot and Ginger Muffins

Prep Time: 10 Mins, Cook Time: 25 Mins, Servings: 12

Ingredients

- 2 cups flour of almond
- 1 tsp each ground cloves, powdered ginger, baking soda
- ½ cup each toasted pecans chopped, shredded coconut unsweetened & melted ghee or nut oil macadamia
- 1 & ½ cups carrot grated
- 3 whisked eggs

Method

- Prepare a 350-degree Fahrenheit oven.
- Whisk together the ginger, cloves, coconut, & baking soda in a medium bowl.
- Eggs, ghee/oil, & Nature Sweet should be mixed in a separate, smaller bowl. Combine the liquids with the dry ones and mix well. Blend in the chopped carrot and nuts.
- Fill muffin cups with the batter & bake for around 20-25 mins.

Nutritional Facts: Calories: 133 Kcal, Protein: 1 g, Carbs: 14 g, Fats: 3 g

6.3 Low-Carb Lemon Coconut Muffins

Prep Time: 05 Mins, Cook Time: 25 Mins, Servings: 12

Ingredients

- 3 lemons Zest & lemons Juice
- ¾ cup flour of almond
- 3 tbsp each baking powder, ground flaxseed & coconut flour
- 3 eggs free-range
- ¼ cup each of coconut oil & coconut cream

Method

- Prepare a 12-cup muffin tray with paper liners & bake at 350°F for 15 mins.
- Mix almond meal, Nature Sweet, flaxseeds, coconut flour, and baking powder in a bowl. Toss in the rest of the ingredients and mix well with a whisk.
- Bake for 15 to 20 mins, or until a toothpick inserted in the center comes out clean. If a skewer inserted into the center of a muffin comes out clean, the muffins are done; if batter remains on the skewer, they need more time in the oven.

Nutritional Facts: Calories: 545 Kcal, Protein: 9 g, Carbs: 70 g, Fats: 24 g

6.4 Walnut and Apricot Balls

Prep Time: 10 Mins, Cook Time: 10 Mins, Servings: 2

Ingredients

- 1 cup apricots dried
- 1 cup walnuts lightly toasted
- 2 tbsps shredded coconut unsweetened
- 1 tbsp seeds chia
- 1 tsp of tahini

Method

- Put the apricots & walnuts in a blender and blend until completely smooth.
- Take it out of the processor and put it onto a serving dish.
- Roll the mix into balls after adding the tahini, coconut, & chia seeds by hand.
- Keep refrigerated.

Nutritional Facts: Calories: 90 Kcal, Protein: 3 g, Carbs: 10 g, Fats: 5 g

6.5 Dairy-Free Strawberry Ice Cream

Prep Time: 10 Mins, Cook Time: 10 Mins, Servings: 2

Ingredients

- 1 cup strawberries frozen
- ½ cup of sugar-free coconut yoghurt full-fat
- ¼ tsp essence vanilla
- ½ tsp sugar substitute Nature Sweet

Method

- Put everything in a blender and whirl it up until it's completely smooth.
- Serve right away, or pop it in the refrigerator if you like your ice cream on the firmer side.

Nutritional Facts: Calories: 209 Kcal, Protein: 0 g, Carbs: 34 g, Fats: 8 g

6.6 Grain-Free Blueberry Muffins

Prep Time: 10 Mins, Cook Time: 25 Mins, Servings: 4

Ingredients

- 3 cups meal almond
- 1 tsp soda baking
- 2 whisked eggs
- ½ cup each of frozen or fresh blueberries & melted coconut oil
- 2 tsps each vanilla extract & sugar alternative Nature Sweet natural

Method

- Turn the oven temperature up to 355.
- The dry ingredients should be combined in a large bowl and stirred carefully.
- In a small bowl, combine the eggs, coconut oil, and vanilla essence and beat with a hand mixer on medium speed for one min.
- Add the egg mixture to the dry ingredients bowl, then mix well by hand. Mix with some blueberries.
- Bake for around 20 mins at 350 degrees or until a toothpick inserted in the center comes out clean.

Nutritional Facts: Calories: 208 Kcal, Protein: 2 g, Carbs: 30 g, Fats: 9 g

6.7 Dairy-Free Pear and Banana Bread

Prep Time: 10 Mins, Cook Time: 20 Mins, Servings: 3

Ingredients

- 1 each soft large pear & overly ripe medium banana
- 3 eggs large
- 1 & ¼ cups meal of almond
- 1/3 cup each of coconut flour & tapioca flour
- ¾ tsp soda (baking)

Method

- Start by preheating the oven to 375°F.
- Bake in a pan lined with nonstick parchment paper.
- Use a food processor to thoroughly combine the banana & pear.
- To your food processor, add the other ingredients, and run on a high speed until completely smooth.
- Bake for 20–25 mins after pouring batter into pan.

Nutritional Facts: Calories: 236 Kcal, Protein: 7 g, Carbs: 25 g, Fats: 14 g

6.8 Sweet Potato Brownies

Prep Time: 10 Mins, Cook Time: 25 Mins, Servings: 4

Ingredients

- 2 & ½ cups grated orange sweet potato
- 2 eggs, whisked
- ½ cup of stevia liquid, cacao powder or cocoa & coconut oil or melted ghee
- 1 tsp almond meal, baking powder, bicarb soda & vanilla extract
- 1/3 cup dried cranberries & toasted slivered almonds

Method

- Start by setting the oven temperature to 365 degrees Fahrenheit.
- Mix the shredded eggs, stevia, sweet potato, and heated ghee or coconut oil in a large dish.
- Put in everything except the almonds & cranberries. Combine thoroughly.
- Mix with the cranberries & almonds, then transfer the batter to a baking pan lined or oiled. Cook for around 25-30 mins. How long you need to bake a sweet potato depends on your oven and how wet your sweet potato is.

Nutritional Facts: Calories: 174 Kcal, Protein: 3 g, Carbs: 21 g, Fats: 9 g

6.9 Gluten-Free Gingerbread Protein Balls

Prep Time: 10 Mins, Cook Time: 20 Mins, Servings: 4

Ingredients

- 1 cup walnuts toasted
- 1 cup almonds roasted
- ½ cup desiccated coconut unsweetened
- 1 tbsp each of chia seeds, ground cloves & ground ginger
- 2 tbsps of honey

Method

- Put everything into a blender and process until it forms a uniform paste.
- If the mixture seems too dry, a splash of water won't hurt. Roll the dough into balls, then place them in a sealed container to chill in the fridge.

Nutritional Facts: Calories: 78 Kcal, Protein: 3.5 g, Carbs: 9 g, Fats: 3 g

6.10 Dessert Baked Pears

Prep Time: 05 Mins, Cook Time: 30 Mins, Servings: 2

Ingredients

- 4 core removed pears
- ¼ cup juice of apple
- 2 tbsps oil of coconut
- 1 tsp extract of vanilla

Method

- Turn the oven temperature up to 400 degrees Fahrenheit.
- Arrange the pear halves, cut side down, in a deep baking dish. Prepare the remaining ingredients by placing them in a small saucepan and heating it over medium heat.
- The pears should be poured with the boiling liquid.
- After the pears have been sliced, place the dish into the oven & bake for around 30 mins.

Nutritional Facts: Calories: 156 Kcal, Protein: 0.6 g, Carbs: 34 g, Fats: 3 g

6.11 Balsamic Roasted Strawberries

Prep Time: 10 Mins, Cook Time: 20 Mins, Servings: 4

Ingredients

- 2 cups strawberries washed & hulled
- 1 tbsp vinegar balsamic
- 1 tbsp sugar coconut
- Greek yogurt

Method

- Put in a preheated 395-degree oven.
- Spread the strawberries in a big, shallow baking dish and sprinkle with the vinegar and sugar. To ensure all strawberries are coated in the mixture, stir it well. The strawberries should rest for 20 mins after being coated.
- Strawberry roasting takes around 10 mins. Top Greek yogurt with them.

Nutritional Facts: Calories: 64 Kcal, Protein: 1 g, Carbs: 11 g, Fats: 3 g

6.12 Low-Carb Chocolate Almond Slice

Prep Time: 10 Mins, Cook Time: 20 Mins, Servings: 12

Ingredients

- 1 cup butter almond
- ½ cup each chopped pecans erythritol xylitol & pastured butter or coconut oil
- 2 tbsps each of baking powder & flour of coconut
- 2/3 cup chocolate chips sugar-free dark & meal almond
- 3 eggs

Method

- Make sure your oven is at 355°F.
- Stir in the coconut oil while the almond butter melts gently. Mix in the erythritol / xylitol.
- Use a fork to whisk the eggs, then add them.
- Replace the chocolate chips with everything else.
- Combine ingredients and transfer to a baking dish. The chocolate chips should be sprinkled on top and carefully pressed into the batter.
- Put in an oven and bake for about 20 mins, till done.

Nutritional Facts: Calories: 277 Kcal, Protein: 6 g, Carbs: 27 g, Fats: 12 g

6.13 5 Min Nectarine Ice-Cream

Prep Time: 05 Mins, Cook Time: 05 Mins, Servings: 2

Ingredients

- 1 cup nectarine pieces chopped, frozen
- 1/3 cup coconut cream canned
- ½ tsp almond or vanilla essence

Method

- Process or blend all ingredients until completely smooth.
- Start serving right now.

Nutritional Facts: Calories: 228 Kcal, Protein: 1 g, Carbs: 25 g, Fats: 13 g

6.14 Dairy-Free Raspberry Ice Cream

Prep Time: 10 Mins, Cook Time: 15 Mins, Servings: 2

Ingredients

- 1 cup raspberries frozen
- ½ cup coconut cream full-fat
- ½ tsp sugar substitute Nature Sweet

Method

- Put everything in a powerful blender and whir it until it's completely smooth.
- Serve right away, or pop it in the refrigerator if you like your ice cream on the firmer side.

Nutritional Facts: Calories: 100 Kcal, Protein: 2 g, Carbs: 21 g, Fats: 2 g

6.15 Crunchy Oat and Nut Bars

Prep Time: 10 Mins, Cook Time: 30 Mins, Servings: 3

Ingredients

- 1 cup Medjool dates pitted fresh
- ¼ cup each of almond butter & maple syrup or honey
- 1 cup pecans, chopped
- 1 & ½ cups oats rolled
- ¼ tsp of salt

Method

- To bring out their flavor and aroma, roast the nuts on a baking sheet coated with foil.
- Make a paste by processing the dates using a food processor.

- Combine everything except the maple syrup/honey & almond butter in a large bowl. Almond butter & honey/maple syrup should be warmed in a small pot until the ingredients are completely blended.

- Add the heated liquid to the container and stir to combine.

- Fill a baking dish with the mixture. Put the mixture in the fridge once you have pressed it down firmly.

- After chilling for 30 mins, the batter may be cut into bars.

Nutritional Facts: Calories: 190 Kcal, Protein: 3 g, Carbs: 29 g, Fats: 7 g

6.16 Dark Chocolate Truffles

Prep Time: 10 Mins, Cook Time: 30 Mins, Servings: 4

Ingredients

- 10 oz chocolate dark

- 3 tbsps oil coconut

- 1 cup coconut milk regular tinned

- ½ cup flaked almonds, crushed

Method

- Piece the chocolate into tiny pieces and add them to the coconut oil in a dish.

- Bring the coconut milk to a boil over high heat in a small saucepan. When the chocolate & coconut oil are melted, add the coconut milk and combine.

- After the mixture has cooled, wrap it in plastic and store it in the freezer for at least 4 hours.

- Make balls from the mixture using the melon baller, then roll them in smashed flaked almonds.

Nutritional Facts: Calories: 170 Kcal, Protein: 2 g, Carbs: 15 g, Fats: 19 g

6.17 Low-Carb Vegan Banana Mug Cake

Prep Time: 10 Mins, Cook Time: 15 Mins, Servings: 1

Ingredients

- ¼ cup banana very ripe, mashed

- 6 tbsps flour of oat

- ½ tsp powder baking

- 1 & ½ tbsps coconut oil melted

- 1 tbsp almonds, flaked

Method

- Start by preheating the oven to 375°F.

- Combine everything and pour it into a oiled cup or ramekin.

- Put it in the oven and let it bake for about 15 mins, till it has puffed up and browned.

Nutritional Facts: Calories: 304 Kcal, Protein: 14 g, Carbs: g, Fats: 20 g

6.18 Gluten-Free Coffee Protein Balls

Prep Time: 10 Mins, Cook Time: 15 Mins, Servings: 2

Ingredients

- 8 pitted Medjool dates
- 1 cup each of cooled coffee & almonds
- ¼ cup of unsweetened cocoa powder or cacao
- 1 tbsp seeds of hemp
- ½ tsp sugar alternative Nature Sweet

Method

- Prepare the coffee by soaking the dates for around 15 mins.
- Put everything in one pot. Put the ingredients in a blender and process till a ball can be formed.

Nutritional Facts: Calories: 109 Kcal, Protein: 4 g, Carbs: 17 g, Fats: 5 g

6.19 Grain Free Cherry Muffins

Prep Time: 5 Mins, Cook Time: 25 Mins, Servings: 2

Ingredients

- 3 cups meal almond
- 1 tsp soda baking
- 2 whisked eggs
- ½ cup melted coconut oil
- ½ cup pitted & chopped cherries, fresh/frozen

Method

- Turn the oven temperature up to 355.
- The dry ingredients should be combined in a medium bowl and stirred carefully.
- Combine the coconut oil, eggs, and sugar (if using) in a medium bowl and beat for one min with a hand mixer.
- Add the egg mixture to the bowl containing the dry ingredients & mix well by hand. Add the cherries and stir well.
- Bake for around 20 mins at 350 degrees or until a toothpick inserted in the center comes out clean.

Nutritional Facts: Calories: 240 Kcal, Protein: 4 g, Carbs: 35 g, Fats: 9 g

6.20 Baked Apples with Cinnamon

Prep Time: 10 Mins, Cook Time: 30 Mins, Servings: 4

Ingredients

- 4 apples medium
- 2 tbsp unsalted pastured butter or coconut oil
- ½ tsp ground cloves
- ¼ cup each of flaked almonds & well-mashed banana
- 3 tbsp of cinnamon & orange juice freshly squeezed

Method

- Put the oven temperature at 350°F.
- Except for the apples & almonds, mix all other ingredients well in a dish.
- Lightly oil a shallow baking dish. Spread some apple slices at the base. Spread the remaining banana mix on top to form a layer. Place the last layer of apple slices on top. Top with almond flakes.
- The apples should be lovely and tender after around 30 minutes inside the oven with the mixture.

Nutritional Facts: Calories: 82 Kcal, Protein: 0.5 g, Carbs: 22 g, Fats: 0.3 g

6.21 Dairy-Free Caramel Ice Cream

Prep Time: 10 Mins, Cook Time: 10 Mins, Servings: 2

Ingredients

- 3 bananas frozen
- 6 large, pitted soft Medjool dates
- 2 tbsps heaped cashew butter
- 2 tbsps coconut cream canned
- 1 tsp essence vanilla

Method

- Combine all ingredients in a blender until a creamy consistency is reached.
- If you want a salted caramel flavor, put some salt over the top before serving.

Nutritional Facts: Calories: 213 Kcal, Protein: 1 g, Carbs: 37 g, Fats: 11 g

6.22 Raw Vegan Pecan Cookies

Prep Time: 10 Mins, Cook Time: 20 Mins, Servings: 2

Ingredients

- 1 cup of pecans
- ¼ cup shredded coconut unsweetened
- ¼ cup cocoa powder or cacao
- 10 pitted Medjool dates

Method

- Put everything in a blender or food processor and run it until it forms a ball and is uniform in texture. A splash of water could help. How wet the dates & nuts are will determine the outcome.
- Make a log using the ingredients and chill in the refrigerator for at least two hours. To serve, cut the log into even rounds of cookies.

Nutritional Facts: Calories: 230 Kcal, Protein: 5 g, Carbs: 28 g, Fats: 12 g

6.23 Dark Chocolate and Blueberry Bites

Prep Time: 10 Mins, Cook Time: 15 Mins, Servings: 2

Ingredients

- 1 cup pecans raw
- ¾ cup Medjool dates pitted
- ½ cup blueberries dried
- 3.5 oz cocoa chopped dark chocolate
- ¼ cup hazelnuts raw

Method

- Start by grinding all of the nuts into a blender or food processor.
- Just before serving, add the other ingredients and pulse to mix.
- Form the dough into balls, then place them in a sealed container to chill in the fridge.

Nutritional Facts: Calories: 52 Kcal, Protein: 0 g, Carbs: 8 g, Fats: 2 g

6.24 Dairy Free Chocolate Pudding

Prep Time: 10 Mins, Cook Time: 15 Mins, Servings: 2

Ingredients

- ¾ cup coconut cream full-fat canned
- ¼ cup sifted cacao powder or cocoa
- 2 tbsps honey or maple syrup
- 1 tbsp seeds chia

- 1 tsp extract of vanilla

Method

- Put everything in a saucepan and cook it over medium. Slowly bring the mix to a simmer while stirring constantly. To get a thicker consistency, continue cooking for a few mins.
- The combination may be served hot or chilled in the refrigerator overnight.

Nutritional Facts: Calories: 100 Kcal, Protein: 1 g, Carbs: 20 g, Fats: 4 g

---

6.25 Sugar-Free Banana Oat Bars
Prep Time: 5 Mins, Cook Time: 30 Mins, Servings: 8

Ingredients

- 2 cups oats rolled
- 2 large, mashed bananas overly ripe
- 1 tsp extract of vanilla
- ¼ cup toasted pecans chopped
- 2 tbsps berries goji

Method

- Start by preheating the oven to 375 degrees F.
- Prepare a lined baking dish.
- Combine everything in a bowl and stir it like crazy.
- Bake for around 30 mins, till gently browned after pouring into a baking dish.

Nutritional Facts: Calories: 180 Kcal, Protein: 3 g, Carbs: 29 g, Fats: 6 g

---

6.26 Watermelon Popsicles
Prep Time: 05 Mins, Cook Time: 20 Mins, Servings: 8

Ingredients

- 1 lb fresh watermelon
- 2 tbsps juice lime
- Maple syrup Stevia, honey

Method

- Put everything in a blender and whirl it up until it's completely smooth.
- The mixture may be strained through a filter to remove any fibrous bits or left as is.
- Fill popsicle molds with the liquid, then set them in the refrigerator to harden.

Nutritional Facts: Calories: 50 Kcal, Protein: 0 g, Carbs: 12 g, Fats: 0 g

6.27 Banana Custard

Prep Time: 10 Mins, Cook Time: 20 Mins, Servings: 2

Ingredients

- 2 well bananas ripened
- 2 dates Medjool
- 9 fluid ozs coconut milk full fat
- 4 large eggs
- 1 tsp essence almond

Method

- Prepare a 350°F oven.
- Mix everything except almond flakes in a high-powered mixer/food processor until smooth. Mix until everything is uniform.
- The mixture should be divided between two oiled baking dishes.
- Put it in the oven and bake for about 20 mins or until it's firm and brown. Your baking time will be different depending on the form of your plates.
- Serve with strawberries & almond flakes.

Nutritional Facts: Calories: 55 Kcal, Protein: 2 g, Carbs: 10 g, Fats: 1.5 g

6.28 Choc Banana Fudge

Prep Time: 10 Mins, Cook Time: 10 Mins, Servings: 2

Crust ingredients

- ½ cup Medjool dates pitted
- 1 cup of walnuts
- ½ cup cacao powder or cocoa

Method

- Use a food blender or high-powered processor to thoroughly mix the crust ingredients. The mixture might need a splash of water if it seems too dry. The answer is conditional on the dates you've used. Distribute the batter in a baking dish that has been prepared in advance.
- Put the topping ingredients in a blender or food processor and pulse until smooth. After spreading the topping on the filling, pop the whole thing in the freezer to set.
- For a cool snack, eat it straight from the freezer or take it out 30 mins before serving.

Nutritional Facts: Calories: 150 Kcal, Protein: 5 g, Carbs: 30 g, Fats: 2 g

6.29 Strawberry Fruit Salad

Prep Time: 10 Mins, Cook Time: 10 Mins, Servings: 4

Ingredients

- 2 cups chopped washed & hulled strawberries
- 2 sliced oranges & chopped kiwi fruits
- 1 sliced large banana
- ¼ cup passionfruit pulp, fresh
- 1 tbsp lime juice fresh

Method

- Gently toss the strawberries, kiwi, oranges, & banana together in a bowl using your hands.
- Combine the passionfruit pulp & lime juice in a blender and drizzle over the salad.
- Toss gently, then dish up.

Nutritional Facts: Calories: 97 Kcal, Protein: 1.4 g, Carbs: 24 g, Fats: 0.5 g

6.30 Warm And Spicy Stewed Apples

Prep Time: 10 Mins, Cook Time: 30 Mins, Servings: 4

Ingredients

- 4 core removed & chopped apples
- 1 tsp cinnamon, ground
- ½ tsp nutmeg, ground
- ¼ tsp ginger, ground
- ¼ cup of water

Method

- Put everything in a saucepan and cook it over low heat until it's about to boil.
- Reduce the heat to low, stir, and let the apples simmer for about 30 mins, till they're very soft.
- Repeat this process if the mixture becomes too dry to stir.
- Add a dollop of coconut cream from a can and serve as a dessert.

Nutritional Facts: Calories: 130 Kcal, Protein: 0 g, Carbs: 32 g, Fats: 1 g

6.31 Chocolate And Hazelnut Fudge

Prep Time: 10 Mins, Cook Time: 25 Mins, Servings: 2

Ingredients

- 7 oz chocolate, dark
- 2 tbsps coconut cream canned full fat
- ¼ cup roasted hazelnuts, chopped

Method

- Combine the coconut cream & melted chocolate. Blend by stirring for a while.
- Hazelnuts should be folded before the batter is poured into tiny muffin patties. To set, chill in the refrigerator.

Nutritional Facts: Calories: 95 Kcal, Protein: 2 g, Carbs: 16 g, Fats: 5 g

6.32 Gluten And Dairy Free Peanut Butter Banana Cake

Prep Time: 05 Mins, Cook Time: 15 Mins, Servings: 3

Ingredients

- 4 whisked eggs & mashed very ripe bananas
- ½ cup each of almond meal & peanut butter
- 4 tbsps softened coconut oil
- ¼ cup chopped pecans
- 1 tsp each of baking powder, baking soda, cinnamon, ground cloves

Method

- Start by preheating the oven to 375 degrees F. Blend or process the mashed bananas, eggs, and peanut butter until smooth. Mix until uniform. Put all the ingredients into a bowl & stir them together well by hand.
- Bake for about an hour, till a toothpick inserted in the center comes out clean, after pouring the mixture into a prepared cake pan.
- Keep the cake in the fridge inside an airtight container.

Nutritional Facts: Calories: 243 Kcal, Protein: 8 g, Carbs: 25 g, Fats: 14 g

6.33 Sugar-Free Coconut Balls

Prep Time: 10 Mins, Cook Time: 30 Mins, Servings: 3

Ingredients

- 2 cups raw cashews
- 1 cup shredded coconut unsweetened
- 2 tbsps oil coconut
- ¼ cup lime juice, fresh

Method

- To make a fine meal out of the cashews, put them through a food processor. Blend the remaining ingredients. More or less lime juice might be preferable. The moisture content of the nuts & coconut you have bought will determine this.
- Roll the dough into balls, then place them in a sealed container to chill in the fridge.

Nutritional Facts: Calories: 131 Kcal, Protein: 3 g, Carbs: 18 g, Fats: 6 g

6.34 Cacao And Almond Smoothie Bowl
Prep Time: 10 Mins, Cook Time: 10 Mins, Servings: 1

Ingredients

- 1 sliced banana frozen
- 1 cup coconut milk
- 1 heaped tbsp almond butter, whey protein and cacao powder
- 2 tbsps of powder
- almonds Flaked

Method

- Everything save the flaked almonds should be blended in a blender until smooth.
- Dish out and top with almond flakes.
- Enjoy

Nutritional Facts: Calories: 628 Kcal, Protein: 14 g, Carbs: 93 g, Fats: 27 g

6.35 Nut Free Bliss Balls
Prep Time: 10 Mins, Cook Time: 10 Mins, Servings: 2

Ingredients

- 6 dates Medjool
- ½ cup raisins & dried apricots
- 1/3 cup seeds hemp
- ½ tsp cinnamon ground
- ¼ tsp nutmeg ground

Method

- Combine all ingredients in a blender or food processor & run until a uniform consistency is reached.
- Roll the dough into balls and store in a sealed jar inside the fridge.

Nutritional Facts: Calories: 312 Kcal, Protein: 2 g, Carbs: 16 g, Fats: 2 g

6.36 Date And Tahini Fudge
Prep Time: 10 Mins, Cook Time: 20 Mins, Servings: 2

Ingredients

- 1 cup of fresh pitted Medjool dates
- ½ cup of tahini
- 2 tbsps oil coconut
- 1-2 tbsps meal almond

Method

- Put everything except the almond meal in a blender or food processor and whisk it until it's smooth and blended.
- Put the concoction in a bowl and take it out. To lessen the mixture's stickiness, add in some almond meal. The dates' moisture content and the tahini's oiliness will determine the final consistency.
- To freeze the mixture, transfer it to a square container.
- Serve by slicing into thin pieces.

Nutritional Facts: Calories: 154 Kcal, Protein: 4 g, Carbs: 15 g, Fats: 4 g

6.37 Baked oranges with coconut cream

Prep Time: 10 Mins, Cook Time: 15 Mins, Servings: 4

Ingredient

- 2 medium oranges
- ¼ cup pecans chopped
- 1 tsp meal almond
- 1 can milk coconut
- ½ tsp essence vanilla

Method

- Prepare a 350°F oven. Cut each orange in half lengthwise.
- Cut the oranges in half and place each half in a muffin cup.
- Combine the almond meal and chopped pecans in a spice or coffee grinder.
- Bake the orange halves with this mixture sprinkled on top. Toast the topping in the oven for 10-15 mins.
- Put the orange halves in the fridge to cool. Bring out the chilled can of coconut milk. Throw away the liquid and transfer the heavy cream to a bowl.
- Put in some vanilla extract. Use electric beaters to whip the coconut milk until it reaches the desired consistency. Serve creamed oranges on orange halves.

Nutritional Facts: Calories: 254 Kcal, Protein: 12 g, Carbs: 28 g, Fats: 11 g

6.38 Chocolate Chia Dessert

Prep Time: 10 Mins, Cook Time: 20 Mins, Servings: 4

Ingredients

- 1 & ½ cups almond or hemp milk
- 1/3 cup slivered almonds, blueberries & seeds, chia
- 3 tbsps carob or cacao powder
- ¼ tsp ground cloves & ground cinnamon
- 10 drops liquid stevia

Method

- Throw everything into a big dish except the berries & pecans. For two mins, beat them with vigor. Leave the ingredients to sit for 5 mins, then give them another min in the whisk.
- Mix in the blueberries and pecans, then divide the mixture into 4 bowls.
- Put the bowls in the refrigerator overnight covered. Use the following day for a meal or a sweet treat.

Nutritional Facts: Calories: 301 Kcal, Protein: 17 g, Carbs: 44 g, Fats: 16 g

6.39 Almond chocolate bark

Prep Time: 15 Mins, Cook Time: 15 Mins, Servings: 4

Ingredients

- 10 oz dark chocolate finely chopped
- 1.5 cups chopped almonds roughly
- 1 tsp ghee or coconut oil

Method

- Prepare a parchment paper-lined rimmed baking sheet. Melt the chocolate and coconut oil together in a double boiler set over just simmering water.
- Spread your chocolate in the pan when it has melted and become smooth.
- Chopped nuts should be sprinkled on top and pressed into the chocolate. The dish should be chilled in the fridge.
- You may serve the bark by breaking it into chunks when it is firm.

Nutritional Facts: Calories: 184 Kcal, Protein: 6 g, Carbs: 13 g, Fats: 2 g

6.40 Sugar-free grilled peaches

Prep Time: 10 Mins, Cook Time: 20 Mins, Servings: 2

Ingredients

- 3 sliced medium peaches
- ¼ cup toasted pecans chopped
- 1 can cream coconut

Method

- Let the coconut milk chill in the fridge all night. The next day, set the peach slices on a grill over medium heat to cook until tender.
- Put the firm coconut cream in a medium bowl by scooping it out of the pan. There's no need to drain the can's contents.
- Blend it into a drink or include it in a curry. The coconut cream may be thickened by whipping it with a hand mixer. Serve the peach halves with a dollop of coconut cream and a sprinkling of nuts.

Nutritional Facts: Calories: 182 Kcal, Protein: 3 g, Carbs: 10 g, Fats: 7 g

6.41 Sugar-Free Cashew Fudge

Prep Time: 10 Mins, Cook Time: 30 Mins, Servings 10

Ingredient

- 1 cup butter cashew
- 1/3 cup coconut oil melted
- 1 tsp extract of vanilla
- ¼ cup cashew pieces roasted

Method

- Process or blend the first 3 ingredients until completely smooth.
- Cashew bits should be stirred into the batter before it is poured onto a prepared baking pan and frozen. To serve, cut into squares.

Nutritional Facts: Calories: 323 Kcal, Protein: 17 g, Carbs: 32 g, Fats: 18 g

6.42 Dairy-Free Strawberry Ice-Cream

Prep Time: 10 Mins, Cook Time: 25 Mins, Servings: 4

Ingredients

- 2 large bananas frozen
- 1 cup strawberries frozen
- ½ cup cream coconut

Method

- Put everything in a powerful processor or food blender and blitz until smooth. Quickly dish it up.

Nutritional Facts: Calories: 287 Kcal, Protein: 19 g, Carbs: 34 g, Fats: 7 g

6.43 Dairy Free Chocolate Popsicles

Prep Time: 10 Mins, Cook Time: 10 Mins, Servings: 6

Ingredients

- 2 cups of coconut milk full fat
- 2 tbsps cocoa powder or cacao
- ½ tsp essence of vanilla
- 10-12 drops liquid stevia

Method

- Combine everything in a wide bowl and whisk until smooth. Use popsicle molds to freeze the mix overnight.

Nutritional Facts: Calories: 404 Kcal, Protein: 20 g, Carbs: 37 g, Fats: 25 g

6.44 Dairy-Free Coconut Custard

Prep Time: 10 Mins, Cook Time: 30 Mins, Servings: 4

Ingredients

- 4 lightly whisked eggs
- 1 cup of canned coconut milk full-fat
- 1 tsp Liquid stevia vanilla extract

Method

- Turn the oven temperature up to 350 degrees Fahrenheit. Put everything (except the eggs) into a small saucepan and cook on low. Never oversteem while using a stove.
- Carefully add the egg mixture to the milk mix and whisk slowly but thoroughly.
- Don't let the ingredients simmer. Fill ramekins with the batter and oil the tops. Prepare a big baking dish with 3/4 water.
- Remove the ramekins from the oven when the custard stops jiggles when shaken. This should take around 30-40 mins. Serve.

Nutritional Facts: Calories: 378 Kcal, Protein: 15 g, Carbs: 37 g, Fats: 8 g

6.45 Chocolate Yogurt Pudding

Prep Time: 10 Mins, Cook Time: 20 Mins, Servings: 2

Ingredients

- 1 & ¼ cups milk nut
- ¼ cup seeds chia

- 3 tbsps Greek yogurt or coconut yogurt & cocoa powder or cacao
- 2 tbsps Nature Sweet goji berries
- cocoa chocolate Shavings

Method

- Put everything in a big dish except the goji berries & chocolate chips.
- Blend them well by whisking. The mixture has to rest for five mins before you whisk it again.
- Place the goji berries into the mixture and divide it between two dishes. Put the custard in dishes and chill them for at least four hours before serving.
- Just before serving, sprinkle some chocolate shavings on top of the puddings.

Nutritional Facts: Calories: 109 Kcal, Protein: 8 g, Carbs: 12 g, Fats: 2 g

6.46 Grain Free Walnut Brownies

Prep Time: 10 Mins, Cook Time: 20 Mins, Servings: 2

Ingredients

- ¼ cup each of almond butter, tapioca flour, almond flour
- 2 whisked eggs
- ½ cup each cacao powder or cocoa & coconut oil melted
- 1 tsp each of baking powder & baking soda
- ½ cup roasted walnuts, chopped

Method

- Put the oven temperature at 350 degrees Fahrenheit.
- Throw everything into a big bowl and stir it with a wooden spoon.
- Bake for around 20 mins after pouring the mixture into a oiled, floured cake and brownie mold.

Nutritional Facts: Calories: 260 Kcal, Protein: 4 g, Carbs: 40 g, Fats: 13 g

6.47 Cacao Chia Banana Pudding

Prep Time: 10 Mins, Cook Time: 10 Mins, Servings: 2

Ingredients

- ¼ cup seeds chia
- 9 oz coconut milk canned
- 2 & ½ tbsps oil coconut & powder of cacao

- 10 drops of stevia
- 1 sliced banana

Method

- Blend some chia seeds, coconut milk, stevia, cacao powder, and sugar. Refine the mixture until it is uniform.
- Put custard in dishes, cover and chill for at least 4 hours, preferably overnight.
- In a skillet, melt the coconut oil over moderate heat. Soften & slightly brown the banana slices in the oven.
- Get out of the fridge the chia puddings. Banana slices & coconut flakes make a delicious topping.
- Serve.

Nutritional Facts: Calories: 200 Kcal, Protein: 4 g, Carbs: 18 g, Fats: 12 g

6.48 No Bake Almond Brownies

Prep Time: 10 Mins, Cook Time: 25 Mins, Servings: 5

Ingredients

- 12 ozs Medjool dates fresh, pitted
- 1 cup of almond flour
- 6 tbsps cacao powder or cocoa
- ½ tsp salt & extract of vanilla
- ¼ cup almonds toasted flaked

Method

- Make use of a food processor to chop up the dates. Run the machine until a ball forms.
- Process until a cohesive mixture forms, then add everything except the flaked almonds. You should be able to push it together with your fingers and have it stay put. If the mixture seems too dry, you may always add more water.
- Spread the mixture into a brownie pan and stir in the flaked almonds.
- To chill before serving, put it in the fridge.

Nutritional Facts: Calories: 213 Kcal, Protein: 5 g, Carbs: 23 g, Fats: 7 g

6.49 Cinnamon Protein Balls

Prep Time: 10 Mins, Cook Time: 10 Mins, Servings: 2

Ingredients

- 1 cup meal almond & shredded coconut unsweetened
- 2 tbsps butter almond
- 5 pits removed Medjool dates

- 1 tsp vanilla extract & ground cinnamon
- 4 tbsps milk of almond

Method

- Put everything in a blender or food processor & blend until smooth. Dates & shredded coconut vary in moisture content, so adjust the quantity of almond milk accordingly.
- Make bite-sized balls from the mixture and keep them in an airtight container in the refrigerator.

Nutritional Facts: Calories: 285 Kcal, Protein: 12 g, Carbs: 19 g, Fats: 19 g

6.50 Dairy-Free Cranberry Chocolate Bark

Prep Time: 10 Mins, Cook Time: 30 Mins, Servings: 3

Ingredients

- ½ cup cacao powder or cocoa
- ½ cup coconut oil, melted
- ¼ cup melted honey
- ¼ cup cranberries dried & pecan pieces, roasted
- Sea salt Generous

Method

- In a bowl, thoroughly combine the first three ingredients.
- Spread the batter on a sheet pan coated with foil or parchment paper. Put a uniform sheen on it.
- The remaining ingredients should be sprinkled equally over the chocolate.
- For best results, chill the tray in the refrigerator for around 30 mins.
- The bark should be broken up and placed in a sealed bag for storage in the fridge.

Nutritional Facts: Calories: 180 Kcal, Protein: 5 g, Carbs: 8 g, Fats: 8 g

Chapter 7: Beverages to Support Liver Health

Here are beverage recipes to purify your liver to regain health and energy.

7.1 Summer Nectarine Smoothie

Prep Time: 5 Mins, Cook Time: 00 Mins, Servings: 2

Ingredients

- 1 nectarine large
- 2 tbsps coconut cream canned
- 1 tbsp flaxseed ground
- 2 tbsps protein powder whey
- 1 & ½ cups water

Method

- Put everything in a blender and whirl it up until it's completely smooth.

Nutritional Facts: Calories: 157 Kcal, Protein: 2 g, Carbs: 40 g, Fats: 0.6 g

7.2 High Protein Blueberry Breakfast Smoothie

Prep Time: 10 Mins, Cook Time: 00 Mins, Servings: 1

Ingredients

- ½ cup of blueberries
- 2 tbsps powder, whey protein
- 1 tbsp hazelnut butter or almond
- 1 & ½ cups of water
- 1 tbsp seeds of hemp

Method

- Put everything in a blender and mix until smooth. Refine the mixture until it is uniform.

Nutritional Facts: Calories: 185 Kcal, Protein: 6 g, Carbs: 36 g, Fats: 1 g

7.3 Infection Fighting Juice

Prep Time: 05 Mins, Cook Time: 00 Mins, Servings: 4

Ingredients

- 1 floret broccoli
- 2 celery sticks
- ½ onion red
- 1 carrot, green apple & clove garlic
- 3 radishes red

Method

- Put everything in a juicer and mix with half a cup of iced green tea for dilution. Get a drink right now!

Nutritional Facts: Calories: 201 Kcal, Protein: 10 g, Carbs: 38 g, Fats: 3 g

7.4 Raw Juice For A Healthy Brain

Prep Time: 15 Mins, Cook Time: 00 Mins, Servings: 1

Ingredients

- ½ cup of blueberries
- ¼ cabbage red
- 1 large carrot & green apple
- 2 radishes red
- 1 parsley large handful

Method

- Use a juicer to make a drink out of all the ingredients.

Nutritional Facts: Calories: 192 Kcal, Protein: 11 g, Carbs: 28 g, Fats: 7 g

7.5 Anti-Inflammatory Raw Juice

Prep Time: 05 Mins, Cook Time: 00 Mins, Servings: 1

Ingredients

- 2-inch slice of pineapple peeled & cored
- 2 celery stalks
- 1 cucumber small
- ½ inch ginger fresh
- 1 large carrot

Method

- Juice everything up in a juicer and enjoy.

Nutritional Facts: Calories: 108 Kcal, Protein: 2 g, Carbs: 13 g, Fats: 1 g

7.6 Vegetable Juice For Edema

Prep Time: 05 Mins, Cook Time: 00 Mins, Servings: 1

Ingredients

- 2 celery stalks
- 1 cucumber small
- 1 parsley large handful
- 1 peeled small lime

- 1-inch fresh ginger

Method

- Put everything in a juicer & drink it.

Nutritional Facts: Calories: 89 Kcal, Protein: 2 g, Carbs: 6 g, Fats: 0.2 g

7.7 Green Smoothie To Detox Your Gallbladder

Prep Time: 10 Mins, Cook Time: 00 Mins, Servings: 1

Ingredients

- 3 handfuls spinach baby
- 1 handful of seeds chia & collard greens beet leaves
- 1 chopped Lebanese cucumber
- ½ sliced banana
- 1 cup coconut milk

Method

- Process or blend all ingredients in a high-powered appliance until completely smooth.

Nutritional Facts: Calories: 132 Kcal, Protein: 6 g, Carbs: 12 g, Fats: 2 g

7.8 Morning Lemon Drink For Detoxing

Prep Time: 05 Mins, Cook Time: 00 Mins, Servings: 1

Ingredients

- 1 mug of warm water
- 2 tbsps lemon juice fresh
- 1 tsp fresh ginger finely grated
- ¼ tsp of salt

Method

- Put everything in a cup and stir. Mix it and take a long drink.
- After eating lemon, it's important to rinse the mouth out with water to get rid of the acid.

Nutritional Facts: Calories: 67 Kcal, Protein: 0 g, Carbs: 12 g, Fats: 0.2 g

7.9 Warm Turmeric Almond Milk

Prep Time: 05 Mins, Cook Time: 00 Mins, Servings: 2

Ingredients

- ½ cup soaked almonds
- 2 cups of water
- ½ inch turmeric slice fresh
- 1 cloves pinch

- Stevia liquid drops

Method

- The almonds should be drained and rinsed well.
- Put everything in a food processor and whirl it up until it's completely smooth.
- Warm the concoction in a saucepan before serving.

Nutritional Facts: Calories: 175 Kcal, Protein: 2 g, Carbs: 16 g, Fats: 1 g

7.10 Alkalizing Green Juice

Prep Time: 10 Mins, Cook Time: 00 Mins, Servings: 3

Ingredients

- 1 large spinach, leaves a handful
- 2 radishes red
- 1 green apple & peeled lime
- 1 large parsley handful
- 1 cucumber medium

Method

- Run everything through a blender, and then drink it.

Nutritional Facts: Calories: 198 Kcal, Protein: 4 g, Carbs: 14 g, Fats: 3 g

7.11 Vegetable Juice For Fluid Retention

Prep Time: 05 Mins, Cook Time: 00 Mins, Servings: 1

Ingredients

- 2 celery stalks
- 1 cucumber medium
- 1 handful parsley & handful spinach
- 1 inch fresh ginger piece
- ½ peeled

Method

- Juice everything up in a juicer and enjoy.

Nutritional Facts: Calories: 45 Kcal, Protein: 2 g, Carbs: 16 g, Fats: 0.3 g

7.12 Bowel Cleansing Smoothie

Prep Time: 05 Mins, Cook Time: 00 Mins, Servings: 1

Ingredients

- 1 & ½ cups seed milk & nut
- 1 tbsp of Fibertone
- 1 tbsp butter almond
- 2 tbsps powder whey protein
- 1 large banana

Method

- Put everything in a food processor & whirl it up until it's completely smooth.

Nutritional Facts: Calories: 170 Kcal, Protein: 12 g, Carbs: 25 g, Fats: 0.3 g

7.13 Gallbladder Cleansing Juice

Prep Time: 05 Mins, Cook Time: 00 Mins, Servings: 1

Ingredients

- 1 each lemon Juice & apple green
- 1 tsp vinegar apple cider
- 2 stalks celery
- 6 beet leaves
- ½ cup tea cold green

Method

- Use a juice extractor to process the apple, leaves, & celery.
- Combine with the rest, and drink. You should then rinse the mouth thoroughly with water to remove any remaining acid and protect your tooth enamel.

Nutritional Facts: Calories: 208 Kcal, Protein: 6.1 g, Carbs: 19.1 g, Fats: 0.5 g

7.14 Cleansing Morning Lemon Drink

Prep Time: 05 Mins, Cook Time: 00 Mins, Servings: 1

Ingredients

- 1 water-warm mug
- 2 tbsps juice fresh lemon
- 1 tsp vinegar apple cider
- ¼ tsp salt

Method

- Put everything in a cup and stir. Mix it and take a long drink.
- To remove the acid from the vinegar and lemon juice from the teeth, it is recommended to rinse the mouth thoroughly with water afterward.

Nutritional Facts: Calories: 109 Kcal, Protein: 3 g, Carbs: 16 g, Fats: 2 g

7.15 Breakfast Peach And Almond Smoothie
Prep Time: 05 Mins, Cook Time: 00 Mins, Servings: 1

Ingredients

- 1 large peach
- 3 tbsps Protein powder
- 1 tbsp almond or cashew butter
- 1 & ½ cups milk of almond

Method

- Put everything in a food processor and whirl until completely smooth.

Nutritional Facts: Calories: 207 Kcal, Protein: 7 g, Carbs: 19 g, Fats: 8 g

7.16 Creamy Peach Smoothie
Prep Time: 05 Mins, Cook Time: 00 Mins, Servings: 1

Ingredients

- 1 peach large
- 2 tbsps powder Protein
- 1 tbsp seeds chia
- 2 tsps flaxseeds/ground linseeds
- 1 & ½ cups of coconut milk

Method

- Put everything in a food processor and whirl it up until it's completely smooth.

Nutritional Facts: Calories: 138 Kcal, Protein: 9.4 g, Carbs: 18 g, Fats: 2.3 g

7.17 Dairy-Free Keto Hot Chocolate
Prep Time: 05 Mins, Cook Time: 00 Mins, Servings: 1

Ingredients

- ½ cup nut milk
- ½ cup of full-fat coconut milk canned
- 1 tbsp cocoa powder unsweetened
- 2 higher cocoa dark chocolate dairy-free
- ½-1 tsp extract of vanilla & sugar alternative Nature Sweet

Method

- Throw everything into a little saucepan. Cook over low heat, stirring constantly, until everything is well combined.
- Put it in a cup you choose and relax.

Nutritional Facts: Calories: 201 Kcal, Protein: 1.3 g, Carbs: 7 g, Fats: 2.2 g

7.18 Immune Boosting Raw Juice

Prep Time: 05 Mins, Cook Time: 00 Mins, Servings: 1

Ingredients

- 2 celery stalks
- ¼ onion red
- 2 leaves cabbage & radishes red
- 1 carrot large
- 2-inch pineapple slice

Method

- Put everything through a juicer and consume.

Nutritional Facts: Calories: 154 Kcal, Protein: 4 g, Carbs: 19 g, Fats: 2.2 g

7.19 Healthy Blood Pressure Juice

Prep Time: 05 Mins, Cook Time: 00 Mins, Servings: 3

Ingredients

- 3 celery stalks
- 6 leaves kale
- 2-inch watermelon slice
- 1 apple red

Method

- Put everything through a juicer and consume. You may cook a lot and store the extra in the freezer.

Nutritional Facts: Calories: 310 Kcal, Protein: 12 g, Carbs: 47 g, Fats: 5 g

7.20 Berry Coconut Smoothie

Prep Time: 05 Mins, Cook Time: 00 Mins, Servings: 1

Ingredients

- 2 tbsps Powder Protein
- ½ cup berries frozen or fresh
- 1 cup of milk
- 1 tbsp coconut cream canned full-fat

Method

- Put everything in a blender and mix until smooth. Put everything in a blender and mix it up, then serve.

Nutritional Facts: Calories: 274 Kcal, Protein: 8 g, Carbs: 39 g, Fats: 1 g

7.21 Banana Papaya Protein Smoothie

Prep Time: 05 Mins, Cook Time: 00 Mins, Servings: 1

Ingredients

- 1 banana small
- 2-inch peeled slice of papaya
- 2 tbsps powder whey protein
- 1 tbsp flaxseeds ground & oil coconut
- 1 & ½ cups of water

Method

- Put everything in a blender & whirl it up until it's completely smooth.

Nutritional Facts: Calories: 209 Kcal, Protein: 2 g, Carbs: 26g, Fats: 1 g

7.22 Chocolate And Hazelnut Protein Smoothie

Prep Time: 05 Mins, Cook Time: 00 Mins, Servings: 1

Ingredients

- 1 chopped frozen banana
- 1 tbsp cocoa powder or cacao & hazelnut butter
- 2 tbsps powder whey protein
- 1 tbsp seeds chia
- 1 glass of milk or water

Method

- Combine everything in a blender and have a good time.

Nutritional Facts: Calories: 198 Kcal, Protein: 17 g, Carbs: 2 g, Fats: 4 g

7.23 Immune Strengthening Juice

Prep Time: 05 Mins, Cook Time: 00 Mins, Servings: 3

Ingredients

- 2 red radishes & sticks celery
- ½ lemon
- 1 carrot
- ¼ onion red

- 1 apple green

Method

- Use a juicer to make a drink out of all the ingredients.

Nutritional Facts: Calories: 323 Kcal, Protein: 16 g, Carbs: 28 g, Fats: 9 g

7.24 Detoxifying Green Smoothie

Prep Time: 05 Mins, Cook Time: 00 Mins, Servings: 1

Ingredients

- 1 peeled orange
- ½ peeled lime
- 2 cups each of coconut milk & baby spinach
- 1 cucumber Lebanese
- 1 tbsp seeds chia

Method

- Put everything except the chia seeds in a high-powered blender & process till smooth. Add chia seeds and give it a good stir.

Nutritional Facts: Calories: 298 Kcal, Protein: 4 g, Carbs: 16 g, Fats: 3 g

7.25 Refreshing Watermelon Juice

Prep Time: 05 Mins, Cook Time: 00 Mins, Servings: 1

Ingredients

- 1 cup watermelon cubed
- 1 handful leaves fresh mint
- 1 cucumber Lebanese
- 1 sliced lime

Method

- Put everything through a juicer and consume.

Nutritional Facts: Calories: 385 Kcal, Protein: 4 g, Carbs: 23 g, Fats: 5 g

7.26 Summer Nectarine Smoothie

Prep Time: 05 Mins, Cook Time: 00 Mins, Servings: 3

Ingredients

- 1 nectarine large
- 2 tbsps coconut cream canned
- 1 tbsp flaxseed ground
- 2 tbsps powder whey protein

- 1 & ½ cups of water

Method

- Put everything in a food processor & whirl it up until it's completely smooth.

Nutritional Facts: Calories: 330 Kcal, Protein: 15 g, Carbs: 36 g, Fats: 4 g

7.27 Gallbladder Cleansing Juice

Prep Time: 05 Mins, Cook Time: 00 Mins, Servings: 1

Ingredients

- 1 peeled medium beet
- 4 leaves beet
- 1 celery stalk
- 2 radishes red
- ½ sliced lemon

Method

- Run the ingredients through a juicer and enjoy.

Nutritional Facts: Calories: 401 Kcal, Protein: 17 g, Carbs: 26 g, Fats: 10.1 g

7.28 Spring Cleanse Juice

Prep Time: 05 Mins, Cook Time: 00 Mins, Servings: 1

Ingredients

- 2 celery stalks
- 1 peeled small beet
- 1 handful of spinach
- 1 apple red
- 1 cucumber Lebanese

Method

- Put everything through a juicer and consume.

Nutritional Facts: Calories: 229 Kcal, Protein: 9.3 g, Carbs: 19.4 g, Fats: 4 g

7.29 Thick And Creamy Strawberry Smoothie

Prep Time: 05 Mins, Cook Time: 00 Mins, Servings: 1

Ingredients

- ½ cup fresh strawberries
- 1 cup hemp or almond milk
- 1 tbsp seeds chia
- 3 tbsps powder whey protein
- 1 tbsp oil coconut

Method

- Put everything in a food processor and whirl it up until it's completely smooth.

Nutritional Facts: Calories: 309 Kcal, Protein: 2 g, Carbs: 37 g, Fats: 4 g

7.30 Liver Loving Beet Juice

Prep Time: 05 Mins, Cook Time: 00 Mins, Servings: 1

Ingredients

- 1 medium peeled beet
- 2 celery stalks
- ½ peeled lemon
- 1 parsley handful

Method

- Put everything through the juicer and consume.

Nutritional Facts: Calories: 198 Kcal, Protein: 3 g, Carbs: 29 g, Fats: 12 g

7.31 High Protein Blueberry Breakfast Smoothie

Prep Time: 05 Mins, Cook Time: 00 Mins, Servings: 1

Ingredients

- ½ cup of blueberries
- 2 tbsps powder whey protein
- 1 tbsp hazelnut or almond butter
- 1 & ½ cups of water
- 1 tbsp seeds of hemp

Method

- Put everything in a food processor and mix until smooth. Refine the mixture until it is uniform.

Nutritional Facts: Calories: 298 Kcal, Protein: 19 g, Carbs: 43 g, Fats: 15 g

7.32 Warm And Spicy Almond Milk

Prep Time: 05 Mins, Cook Time: 00 Mins, Servings: 1

Ingredients

- 1 cup milk, almond
- ½ tsp ground cinnamon & ground turmeric
- 1 pinch cloves ground
- 1 nutmeg pinch
- 1 tsp oil coconut

Method

- Warm the milk made from almonds in a saucepan. Add the rest of the ingredients and whisk to combine when it reaches a simmer.

Nutritional Facts: Calories: 87 Kcal, Protein: 5 g, Carbs: 8 g, Fats: 1 g

7.33 Healthy Gallbladder Juice

Prep Time: 05 Mins, Cook Time: 00 Mins, Servings: 1

Ingredients

- 8 leaves beet
- ½ peeled beet
- 2 radishes red & celery stalks
- 1 handful leaves arugula
- 1 peeled lime

Method

- Put everything through a juicer and consume.

Nutritional Facts: Calories: 98 Kcal, Protein: 6 g, Carbs: 10.1 g, Fats: 0.4 g

7.34 Refreshing Watermelon Smoothie

Prep Time: 05 Mins, Cook Time: 00 Mins, Servings: 1

Ingredients

- 1 cup watermelon cubes fresh
- ½ lime Juice
- 1 tbsp seeds chia
- 1 frozen banana chopped
- ½ cup hemp or nut milk

Method

- Put everything in a food processor and whirl it up until it's completely smooth.

Nutritional Facts: Calories: 164 Kcal, Protein: 9 g, Carbs: 32 g, Fats: 7 g

---

7.35 Immune Boosting Raw Juice

Prep Time: 05 Mins, Cook Time: 00 Mins, Servings: 3

Ingredients

- 1 piece fresh ginger peeled
- ¼ onion red
- 1 each stick celery, peeled orange & large carrot
- ¼ lime peeled
- 6 leaves kale

Method

- Put everything through a juicer and consume.

Nutritional Facts: Calories: 201 Kcal, Protein: 3 g, Carbs: 22 g, Fats: 5 g

---

7.36 Clean Green Smoothie

Prep Time: 05 Mins, Cook Time: 00 Mins, Servings: 1

Ingredients

- 1 cucumber Lebanese
- 1 banana & handful leaves of baby spinach
- ½ zucchini medium
- 2 tbsps coconut oil & hemp seeds
- 1 cup milk hemp

Method

- Put everything in a high-powered blender and whir until it's completely smooth.

Nutritional Facts: Calories: 403 Kcal, Protein: 14 g, Carbs: 26 g, Fats: 11 g

---

7.37 Creamy Cantaloupe Smoothie

Prep Time: 05 Mins, Cook Time: 00 Mins, Servings: 1

Ingredients

- ½ cup coconut milk, canned & full fat
- ½ cup of water
- 2 tbsps powder whey protein
- 1 cup of cantaloupe diced
- 2 tbsps seeds chia

Method

- Put everything in a blender and whirl it up until it's completely smooth.

Nutritional Facts: Calories: 265 Kcal, Protein: 3 g, Carbs: 27 g, Fats: 4 g

7.38 Choc Mint Protein Smoothie

Prep Time: 05 Mins, Cook Time: 00 Mins, Servings: 1

Ingredients

- 1 & ½ cups milk
- 3 tbsps powder whey protein
- 1 tbsp cacao powder or cocoa
- 1 drop peppermint oil essential
- 1 tbsp seeds chia

Method

- Blend all the ingredients in a food processor until they are completely combined.

Nutritional Facts: Calories: 322 Kcal, Protein: 18 g, Carbs: 45 g, Fats: 23 g

7.39 Cleansing Red Juice

Prep Time: 05 Mins, Cook Time: 00 Mins, Servings: 1

Ingredients

- 1 peeled medium beet
- ¼ cup blueberries fresh/frozen
- 1 large carrot
- 4 leaves cabbage red

Method

- Put everything through a juicer and consume.

Nutritional Facts: Calories: 104 Kcal, Protein: 2 g, Carbs: 15 g, Fats: 1 g

7.40 Creamy Pumpkin Smoothie

Prep Time: 05 Mins, Cook Time: 00 Mins, Servings: 1

Ingredients

- ½ cup pumpkin cooked mashed
- 2 tbsps powder whey protein
- 1 tbsp each almond butter & chia seeds
- ¼ tsp powdered pumpkin spice
- 1 & ½ cups coconut milk or water

Method

- Put everything in a food processor and whirl it up until it's completely smooth.

Nutritional Facts: Calories: 189 Kcal, Protein: 12 g, Carbs: 33 g, Fats: 6 g

7.41 Kidney Cleansing Juice

Prep Time: 05 Mins, Cook Time: 00 Mins, Servings: 3

Ingredients

- 2 celery stalks
- 1 large parsley handful
- 1 peeled orange
- 1 cucumber Lebanese
- 6 leaves lettuce

Method

- Juice everything up in a juicer and enjoy.

Nutritional Facts: Calories: 112 Kcal, Protein: 6 g, Carbs: 19 g, Fats: 3 g

7.42 Creamy Mango And Banana Smoothie

Prep Time: 05 Mins, Cook Time: 00 Mins, Servings: 1

Ingredient

- half mango Flesh
- 1 frozen banana chopped
- 1 & ½ cups milk coconut
- 1 tsp oil coconut
- 2 tbsps powder whey protein

Method

- Put everything in a food processor and whirl it up until it's completely smooth.

Nutritional Facts: Calories: 156 Kcal, Protein: 3 g, Carbs: 13 g, Fats: 1 g

7.43 Cleansing Green Juice

Prep Time: 05 Mins, Cook Time: 00 Mins, Servings: 1

Ingredients

- 1 green apple, level scoop powder & Lebanese cucumber
- 2 radishes red
- 2-inch watermelon slice
- 1 large parsley handful
- 6 leaves kale

Method

- Use a juice extractor on all of the produce.
- Blend Ultimate powder with fruit juice.

Nutritional Facts: Calories: 221 Kcal, Protein: 16 g, Carbs: 34 g, Fats: 12.2 g

7.44 Chia And Yogurt Smoothie

Prep Time: 05 Mins, Cook Time: 00 Mins, Servings: 1

Ingredients

- 2 tbsps Greek yogurt full fat
- 1 tbsp seeds chia
- ½ cup fresh strawberries
- 1 cup milk nut
- 2 tbsps powder whey protein

Method

- Put everything in a food processor and whirl it up until it's completely smooth.

Nutritional Facts: Calories: 398 Kcal, Protein: 19 g, Carbs: 54 g, Fats: 21 g

7.45 Creamy Peach Smoothie

Prep Time: 05 Mins, Cook Time: 00 Mins, Servings: 1

Ingredients

- 1 peach large
- 1 tbsp cream coconut
- 2 tbsps powder whey protein
- 1 tbsp seeds chia
- 1 & ½ cups of milk

Method

- Blend all the ingredients in a food processor until they are completely combined.

Nutritional Facts: Calories: 570 Kcal, Protein: 8 g, Carbs: 116 g, Fats: 11 g

Conclusion: Staying Committed to Liver Health

As you wrap up your journey through the "Fatty Liver Cookbook," it's crucial to emphasize the importance of continued commitment to liver health beyond the pages of this book. Staying dedicated to maintaining a healthy liver is an ongoing process that requires vigilance, self-awareness, and a proactive approach.

Tracking Progress

One of the keys to success in managing fatty liver disease is monitoring your progress. Keeping track of your dietary choices, lifestyle changes, and overall well-being can help you make informed decisions and stay motivated. Here's how you can effectively track your progress.

Seeking Medical Advice

While this cookbook provides valuable insights and guidance, it's essential to remember that fatty liver disease is a medical condition that should be managed in consultation with healthcare professionals. Here's why seeking medical advice is crucial.

In conclusion, staying committed to liver health is a lifelong journey that requires dedication, patience, and continuous learning. By tracking your progress, seeking regular medical advice, and making informed choices, you can take charge of your liver health and work towards a healthier, happier future. Remember that you have the power to make a positive impact on your liver and overall well-being, and your commitment to a liver-friendly lifestyle is a step in the right direction.

Resources and References

In your journey to better liver health, it's essential to have access to credible sources of information, support, and further guidance. This section provides a compilation of valuable resources and references to help you continue exploring and understanding fatty liver disease and its management.

1. Online Resources:

- **American Liver Foundation (ALF):** The ALF website (**www.liverfoundation.org**) provides a wealth of information on liver health, including educational articles, patient resources, and support groups.

- **National Institute of Diabetes and Digestive and Kidney Diseases (NIDDK):** NIDDK (**www.niddk.nih.gov**) offers valuable insights into liver diseases, including NAFLD, with a focus on research and clinical guidelines.

- **Mayo Clinic:** Mayo Clinic's website (**www.mayoclinic.org**) features informative articles on liver diseases, symptoms, and lifestyle recommendations for managing fatty liver disease.

2. Support Groups and Communities:

- **Reddit's r/fatty liver:** An online community where individuals share their experiences, questions, and support related to fatty liver disease.

- **Local Support Groups:** Check with your local healthcare providers or hospitals for information on support groups in your area dedicated to liver health.

3. Healthcare Providers:

- Consult your primary care physician, hepatologist, or gastroenterologist for personalized guidance and medical advice related to your liver health needs.

4. Medical Journals and Research:

- Stay informed about the latest advancements in liver health by exploring medical journals such as "Hepatology," "Liver International," and "Clinical Liver Disease."

5. Government Health Agencies:

- The Centers for Disease Control and Prevention (CDC) and the World Health Organization (WHO) offer authoritative information on liver diseases, including risk factors, prevention, and global health initiatives.

Remember to use these resources as tools to empower yourself with knowledge, support, and inspiration on your journey to optimal liver health. Always verify information from reputable sources and consult with healthcare professionals for personalized advice and guidance tailored to your unique needs and circumstances. Your commitment to liver health is a vital step toward a healthier and happier life.

Measurement Conversion Table

CUP	OUNCES	MILLILITERS	TABLESPOONS
8 cup	64 oz.	1895 ml	128
6 cup	48 oz.	1420 ml	96
5 cup	40 oz.	1180 ml	80
4 cup	32 oz.	960 ml	64
2 cup	16 oz.	480 ml	32
1 cup	8 oz.	240 ml	16
3/4 cup	6 oz.	177 ml	12
2/3 cup	5 oz.	158 ml	11
1/2 cup	4 oz.	118 ml	8
3/8 cup	3 oz.	90 ml	6
1/3 cup	2.5 oz.	79 ml	5.5
1/4 cup	2 oz.	59 ml	4
1/8 cup	1 oz.	30 ml	3
1/16 cup	1/2 oz.	15 ml	1

Dear Valued Customers,

I am thrilled to present you with an exclusive opportunity to enhance your cooking experience with my cookbook! As a token of our appreciation for your support, I invite you to download a complimentary PDF containing all the mouthwatering images of our recipes. Simply scan the QR code below to access this delightful addition to your culinary journey.

🔍 Four Reasons to Download the PDF:

Enhanced Visual Experience: By accessing the PDF, you'll enjoy high-quality images of each recipe, showcasing the vibrant colors, textures, and presentation details that truly bring our dishes to life. With crisp, detailed visuals at your fingertips, you can better visualize your culinary creations and inspire your cooking adventures.

Convenience and Accessibility: Unlike traditional cookbooks, where space constraints may limit the number of images included, our separate PDF ensures that you have access to every recipe's visual representation. Whether you're planning your next meal at home or browsing for inspiration on the go, having a digital copy of the images provides unparalleled convenience and accessibility.

Cost Efficiency: Printing high-quality images directly in the cookbook significantly increases production costs, which ultimately leads to higher purchasing prices for our customers. By offering a separate PDF for the recipe images, we can maintain an affordable price point for the cookbook while still providing you with stunning visuals to complement your cooking experience.

Personalization and Sharing: The PDF format empowers you to personalize your cooking experience. Easily print out your favorite recipe images for your kitchen inspiration board or see it in your tablet or mobile while cooking. With the ability to save, print, and share the images, you can spread the joy of cooking and create lasting memories with loved ones.

⌨ Scan the QR Code Below to Get Started:

Thank you for choosing my cookbook to accompany you on your culinary adventures. I hope this additional resource enriches your cooking journey and inspires countless delicious meals in your kitchen.

Enjoyed Our Cookbook? Leave a Review on Amazon! If you've enjoyed my cookbook and the complimentary gift of recipe images, I would greatly appreciate it if you could take a moment to leave a positive review on Amazon. Your feedback helps me continue to provide excellent resources and inspires others to discover the joy of cooking with my recipes.

Happy cooking!

Alex Mc Corner

Printed in Great Britain
by Amazon

40959062R00071